THE
POCKET BOOK
OF
ARSENAL

By Kevin Whitcher

With special thanks to Brian Dawes

Published by Vision Sports Publishing in 2009

Vision Sports Publishing
19-23 High Street
Kingston upon Thames
Surrey
KT1 1LL

www.visionsp.co.uk

Text © Kevin Whitcher
Illustrations © Bob Bond Sporting Caricatures

ISBN: 978-1905326-63-1

Series editor: Jim Drewett
Series production: Martin Cloake
Design: Neal Cobourne
Illustrations: Bob Bond
Cover photography: Paul Downes, Objective Image
All pictures: Getty Images

Printed and bound in Italy by Graphicom SRL

A CIP catalogue record for this book is available from the British Library

THIS IS AN UNOFFICIAL PUBLICATION

All statistics in *The Pocket Book of Arsenal* are correct up until the start
of the 2009/10 season.

CONTENTS

FOREWORD BY
GEORGE GRAHAM

As a player, it was a very big culture shock joining Arsenal from Chelsea when I did in 1966. I came to a much bigger club, although underperforming, but I began to understand what professionalism they stood for, with very high standards. Twenty years later when I became manager I was ecstatic at getting the job and as I settled, realised the important position I held, looking around the place. It was full of successful history. Also, as I did a lot of travelling in the job, I had time to enjoy reading and learning about the history of the club and I built up a decent collection of old Arsenal books, going back to those written by Herbert Chapman, George Allison and David Jack.

I learned that the Gunners were one of the first English clubs to travel regularly abroad, including South America, and that Arsenal don't do things on the cheap. The stadium they built at Highbury was way ahead of its time with the two main stands, the Marble Halls and the standards of the dressing rooms. And that was back in the days before the Second World War, when it was unbelievable to think that visiting teams could come and play in this magnificent stadium. And what they've done over the last few years is the same again, building a home that is arguably the best in Great Britain and probably Europe.

I can't help but be proud of my own part in the club's history, and I wanted to win as many trophies as I could in my time as manager at Arsenal. But it was hard to think anyone could come close to what Herbert Chapman did at the club. He was ahead of his time with changes such as the white sleeves, numbers on shirts, floodlights and getting the name of the local underground station changed to Arsenal.

I am sure readers will delight in either reminiscing in or learning about the triumphs in the rich history of the club, including those in which I played a part, such as the 1971 double and the great nights at Anfield and in Copenhagen.

But to finish, I think it's time to lay to rest a myth that has grown since my days as the boss at Highbury. One day I was playing games with journalists and I told them that, being a keen gardener, when I planted my bulbs for the following spring, I placed the tulips to grow in a 4-4-2 formation and the daffodils in a 3-5-2. On a roll, I then told them I was having a swimming pool put in, with the Arsenal crest and the cannon inlaid into the tiles on the bottom! They printed it and people believed it. So much so that even now, it's amazing when people come round and they still ask to see the famous swimming pool!

So although you can't believe everything you read in the newspapers, the same cannot be said of the great story of a very special football club you will read about on the pages that follow. Enjoy.

Special thanks to George Graham, his fee for this foreword has been donated to Bob Wilson's Willow Foundation.

...CLUB DIRECTORY...

Club address: Arsenal Football Club
Highbury House, 75 Drayton Park
London N5 1BU

General club enquiries: 020 7619 5003

Fax Number: 020 7704 4001

Box Office/Ticket Info: 020 7619 5000

Dial-a-Ticket: 0844 277 3625

Match Information Line: 0844 931 2211

Stadium Tours: 020 7619 5000

Junior Gunners: 020 7619 5000

Travel Club: 020 7619 5000

Commercial & Marketing: 020 7704 4170

Corporate Hospitality:
0845 262 0001

Highbury House
Restaurant:
020 7704 4270

The Armoury Shop:

    020 7704 4120

All Arsenal Shop: 020 7704 4128

Arsenal Shop at Finsbury Park:

    020 7272 1000

Arsenal Home Shopping:

    020 7619 5000

Arsenal Soccer Schools: 020 7704 4140

Arsenal in the Community: 020 7704 4140

Disability Helpline: 020 7619 5050

Arsenal Ladies: 01727 747 452

Email addresses:

General Enquiries:

    info@arsenal.co.uk

Box Office: boxoffice@arsenal.co.uk

Membership:

    membership@arsenal.co.uk

Club website: www.arsenal.com

THE STORY OF THE GUNNERS
EARLY BATTLES
1886-1924

When Arsenal began their illustrious history in 1886, they were effectively a works team. Four friends employed at Royal Arsenal, a government munitions factory in Woolwich, south east London, decided to form the club and named it after Dial Square, one of the factory's workshops.

David Danskin was the main organiser of the quartet and raised the ten shillings and sixpence required for a football by getting some of his workmates to chip in with sixpence each. Danskin was also the club's first captain and a debut match was arranged against Eastern Wanderers. The Dial Square players provided their own kits, albeit ones of different colours. The factory was a good source of players and the opposition were beaten 6-0. This despite the pitch being somewhat unorthodox by modern standards, its shape dictated by the surrounding backyards and a ditch that was little more than an open sewer.

The team held a meeting at the Royal Oak public house soon after and agreed two significant changes. The club's name would be Royal Arsenal and their home games would be played on Plumstead Common. The nearby Star pub was used for their changing rooms, and although times moved on, a century later the concept of an Arsenal player being in a public house in the build-up to a match was not unheard of until the arrival of Arsène Wenger as manager.

The team improved as some of the factory workers Danskin recruited had experience of playing at a higher level for clubs in both England and Scotland. The 1890 London Charity Cup provided Arsenal's first

Fans stream away from the main gate at the club's ground in Woolwich, south east London, 1912

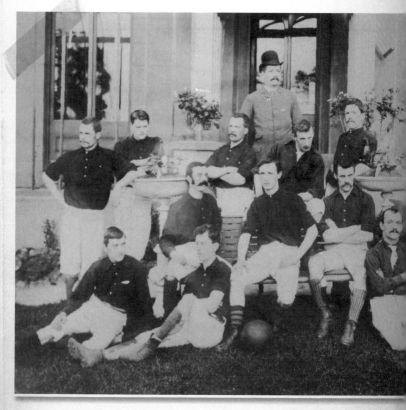

One of the earliest pictures of the club, then called Royal Arsenal, in 1888

trophy, and a year later the club changed their name again, to Woolwich Arsenal.

Arsenal first entered the FA Cup in 1892, only to be knocked out by Derby County. To rub salt in the wound, Derby promptly signed two of Arsenal's

players at the end of the game! Derby were a first division team, which left the non-league amateurs of Arsenal powerless to prevent the players from leaving – all this a hundred years before anyone had heard of Jean-Marc Bosman.

The affair prompted the club to apply to join the Football League, and the application was accepted. Their first season as a fully-fledged professional league club was spent in the second division in 1893, ending with a ninth-place finish. By this time, they had moved to Plumstead's Invicta Ground, where they had been playing for three years. When its owner upped the annual rent from £200 to £350 as Arsenal's success grew, the club decided to buy their own ground and formed a limited liability company to raise the money to buy the Manor Ground, nearby in Plumstead. The 1,552 £1 shares were mostly bought by manual workers who lived in the local area, with not a billionaire in sight.

In 1904, less than 20 years after their formation, the team won promotion to the First Division. By this time, they were enjoying sizeable crowds, with over 25,000 turning up for one FA Cup tie. However, the club failed to push on due to financial problems, and were forced to sell some of their better players. In 1913 they eventually paid the price and were relegated back to Division Two. By this time, property magnate Sir Henry Norris had become the chairman, and felt the club needed to move to a highly populated area with a good transport network. He agreed with the Church of England to buy a 21-year lease on some land they owned in Highbury, north London, very close to the Gillespie Road underground station. Despite opposition from Tottenham, Leyton Orient

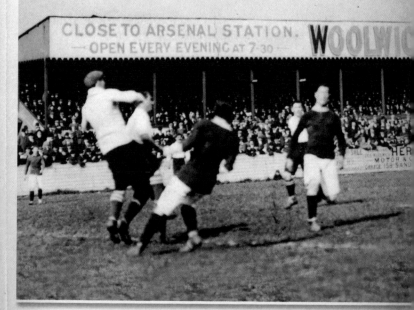

and Chelsea, the Football League decided there was nothing in their rules to prevent the move, so Arsenal became a north London club, and are still regarded as arrivistes by Spurs fans to the current day.

Aside from the £20,000 cost of the lease, Norris paid £80,000 to build a stadium on the land. He needed the club to return to the top division if he was to profit from his investment. This was managed when League football resumed in 1918 after the First World War, although Arsenal's promotion to an expanded First Division was somewhat controversial, as they

An early clash with Spurs, in the 1906 Southern Charity Cup, at the Manor Ground in Plumstead

returned due to a vote amongst the league chairmen
rather than their pre-war finishing position. That it
was at the expense of near neighbours Tottenham
Hotspur, who were relegated to Division Two at
the same time, made the questionable nature of the
Gunners' rise to the top flight all the sweeter. The
club have never suffered relegation since.

Leslie Knighton was appointed manager in
1919, but enjoyed limited success, eventually being
sacked by Norris six years later after the club had
narrowly avoided relegation. His job was advertised
in *Athletic News*, the description culminating in the
words, "Gentlemen whose sole ability to build up
a good side depends on the payment of heavy and
exorbitant transfer fees need not apply." Early in the
club's history, the notion of seeing good players leave
and there being limited funds to build the team was
already becoming familiar to Arsenal fans…

However, when the crunch came, Henry Norris
realised that he had to speculate to accumulate – as
he had done with the building of the stadium in
Highbury. So he paid the successful manager of
Huddersfield Town, Herbert Chapman, handsomely
to head south and leave behind the club where he
had won two league titles in succession (a third
was added by the team he had built). Norris had a
reputation as something of a dictator, as Knighton
wrote, "Everyone was afraid of Sir Henry. And
no wonder! I have never met his equal for logic,
invective and ruthlessness against all who opposed

him." Chapman, aware of this, bargained hard before agreeing to take the job, and insisted on complete control over team matters as well as money to strengthen the squad. Things were going to be done differently under the new manager.

Huddersfield pinned in defence during an early game at Highbury

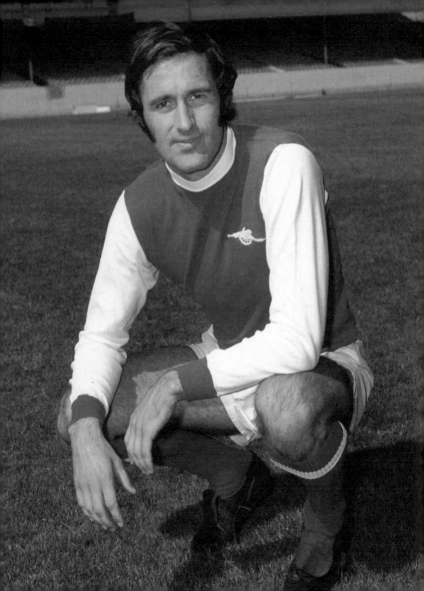

BADGE OF
HONOUR

Arsenal's first crest came into existence two years after the club was formed, and was very similar to the coat of arms of the borough of Woolwich in which they played, which also featured lions' heads and three upright cannons.

The club's very first crest, inspired by the Borough of Woolwich's coat of arms

The area was synonymous with the military, so it was not only its formation by workers in the Royal Arsenal armaments factory that was a factor in the choice of design. Cannons were dropped from the crest when the move to a new home north of the river took place in 1913, but only for nine years. Given the club's nickname continued to be The Gunners, it was hardly surprising that they did not remain absent for long.

The version seen on the 1935 shirt was one of several variations on the theme of a single cannon with the AFC lettering, as the crest seemed to be tweaked on an almost annual basis in the 1920s and 30s. Initially, the cannon pointed eastwards, although over the years fans were to become familiar with the westward direction seen on the 1930s versions. The frequent changes were not a cause of great controversy because the crest was rarely featured on the players' shirts except on special occasions such as

cup finals. It tended to be more a feature of the club's stationary and matchday programmes.

One version from this time that has remained popular to this day is the one which became a feature of the newly rebuilt East Stand in 1936. It was inlaid on the first floor of the stadium's Marble Halls reception, in the lobby that led to the directors' box, as well as featuring above the doorway on the exterior of the listed building. Forming the letters 'AFC', the club continue to use this on their merchandising today. The cannon had not been ignored in the design though, as this was inlaid on the floor on the ground floor and also featured outside on the façade of the art deco stand.

A new crest was unveiled in 1949 that featured the Latin motto 'Victoria Concordia Crescit' (which translates as 'victory grows out

Captain Tom Parker in 1930, with one of a number of badge designs from the era

The 1936 crest, still in evidence today

of harmony'). The design also featured the London Borough of Islington's coat of arms and the word 'Arsenal' picked out in gothic lettering. It was used for 53 years, experiencing only minor changes – mainly the colours of the various elements.

On the players' shirts, as a crest became a constant rather than occasional feature, the design was reduced to a simple cannon, as much because it was stitched in rather than being a sewn on badge. Uniformity of the official club crest and what was on the team shirts did not occur until 1990.

Adopted in 1949, this famous crest lasted 53 years and became synonymous with the club

In 2001, the club embarked on a long-running legal case against a street trader outside the stadium who sold souvenirs with the club's crest on, and there was much debate in the courts over the legal ownership of the club's historical crests as trademarks.

The stripped down cannon that adorned the classic shirt of the 1970s, modelled by Charlie George

Before the case was resolved, and due to

the confusion over the many different variations of the design over the course of its history ("It's very difficult to track back the origin of the crest and was difficult to copyright" admitted vice-chairman David Dein) the club decided to ensure that in the future there would be no scope for debate by introducing a completely new version for the 2002/03 season.

Rather than warn fans of the plans to make the change, the club – having trialed ideas before a very limited number of focus groups – unveiled the crest before a home league match early in 2002. Having announced the new design the day before, a flag bearing it was carried around the pitch to be received by a chorus of boos from the Highbury crowd. Chairman Peter Hill-Wood might have stated, "I would like to stress that this change is an evolution not a revolution", but there was revolt in the air.

It was not a good start, but the new version came to be accepted in time and is now writ large on the exterior of the new Emirates stadium. The cannon points east once again whilst the Latin motto has been dispensed with. With a much cleaner design, in contrast to its predecessors, it is unlikely to see any major changes.

The initially unpopular new design, unveiled in 2002

THE INVINCIBLES

The undefeated, heavyweight champions of England parade the trophy in Islington

Between defeats to Leeds United on 4th May 2003 and Manchester United on 24th October 2004, Arsenal set a new English record of 49 consecutive unbeaten league matches. The previous best of 42, set by Brian Clough's Nottingham Forest, had spanned two seasons but did not include a complete campaign without defeat as Arsenal astonishingly achieved over the 38 fixtures of the 2003/04 Premiership season.

The team was known variously as the '49ers', the 'Unbeatables' and the 'Invincibles', after surpassing Forest's record. Clough himself described Arsenal as "nothing short of incredible," adding that they "caress a football the way I dreamed of caressing Marilyn Monroe." And it was the style with which they set the record that enhanced the achievement. A major statistical feat in itself, but to do it playing the type of football that often had opposition fans applauding them off the

field made it more remarkable still. And it became more difficult to maintain the longer it went on. "We will be a big trophy for the first team that beats us," said Wenger when the run reached 40 matches. "Every team that plays Arsenal will treat it like a cup game."

It was achieved at a time when Chelsea were spending tens of millions in the transfer market to compete with both the Highbury-based club and Manchester United (no one else had won the title for nine seasons). Such was the finance-fuelled revolution at Stamford Bridge that only something like an unbeaten season could prevent them usurping the status quo, as the subsequent two campaigns proved.

Three architects of success; icon, captain and manager

On finishing the 2003/04 league programme without a defeat, Wenger admitted, "at the beginning of this season I never felt we were capable of remaining unbeaten. I knew Chelsea had big buys and Manchester United had strengthened, and never expected us to do it."

The sequence – of 36 wins and 13 draws – was the pinnacle of four seasons in which Arsenal enjoyed five major trophies, and with only Jens Lehmann added to the 2002/03 squad of players, it proved that spending big was not always the way to achieve success. Wenger had little choice, as his budget was severely restricted by the club's need to put any income they could garner towards the building of their new stadium. The last summer in which he was able to splash significant cash was in 2001.

The Invincibles team succeeded because they mixed experience, skill,

In a great season of great performances, Henry's contribution was arguably the greatest of all pace, flexibility and an almost telepathic understanding. All the players could chip in with goals and were comfortable in possession. The first choice eleven of Lehmann, Lauren, Toure, Campbell, Cole, Ljungberg, Vieira, Gilberto, Pires, Bergkamp and Henry was supplemented by some excellent back-up such as Keown, Parlour, Edu, Kanu and Wiltord. All international players that fitted in seamlessly when called upon. The only strengthening Wenger needed to do midway through the run was the purchase of Jose Antonio Reyes, with Wiltord out injured for several months.

"I always had that dream, and to fulfil it is marvellous," said Wenger of the unbeaten season

The players demonstrated great team spirit, both early in the run at Manchester United, when they found themselves unjustly reduced to ten men after the dismissal of Patrick Vieira but survived a last minute penalty to take a point, and at home to Liverpool several months later. Having suffered exits from the FA Cup and the Champions League in the previous week at the hands of United and Chelsea, they found themselves 2-1 down at half time and could see their title assault slipping away. In the following 45 minutes, they rallied, and won 4-2. These were both games where immense mental fortitude proved to be invaluable in the making of the Invincibles.

ARSENAL COMIC STRIP HISTORY 1

1987... IT IS HALF-TIME IN THE LEAGUE CUP SEMI-FINAL SECOND LEG AT SPURS. ARSENAL ARE 0-2 DOWN ON AGGREGATE...

WE CAN STILL TURN THIS AROUND...

AS MANAGER GEORGE GRAHAM SPEAKS, THE PLAYERS CAN HEAR THE SPURS PA ANNOUNCER...

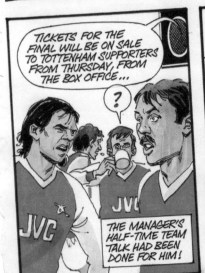

TICKETS FOR THE FINAL WILL BE ON SALE TO TOTTENHAM SUPPORTERS FROM THURSDAY, FROM THE BOX OFFICE...

?

THE MANAGER'S HALF-TIME TEAM TALK HAD BEEN DONE FOR HIM!

THE GUNNERS DREW LEVEL IN THE SECOND HALF BEFORE GOING ON TO WIN THE REPLAY, WITH 'ROCKY' ROCASTLE SCORING THE WINNER.

GOAL!

CUP FINAL TICKETS WENT ON SALE FROM A BOX OFFICE THREE MILES SOUTH WEST OF WHITE HART LANE!

STADIUMS

Arsenal have had several grounds in

their history, but the one they called 'home' for the majority of the club's existence – from 1913 until 2006 – was officially known as 'The Arsenal Stadium'. It was rarely referred to as anything but 'Highbury' after the area of its location.

Sir Henry Norris, the chairman in 1913, re-located the club from south east London due to the urgent need to increase income. Plumstead was a tiresome journey from central London with difficult transport links, whereas Highbury was not only served by three major railway lines but also in the midst of a much better catchment area of football fans than the south east outskirts. Many local residents objected to the plan, and nothing has changed in this regard, although today it can be claimed that most of them moved to the area after Arsenal Football Club so knew what to expect.

The new stadium, built on land leased from St John's College of Divinity, was designed by Archibald Leitch, the leading stadium designer of his day. Initially, Highbury featured only one wooden stand – on the east side, with the other three sides being banked terracing. The club bought the land outright in 1925, and built a magnificent Art Deco-style stand designed by Claude Ferrier on the west side in 1932. Soon after, the existing East Stand was demolished so that a similar one could be built to match that opposite, and subsequently the two stands were designated listed buildings due to their architectural importance.

The ends were not entirely neglected, with a roof being added to the re-terraced Laundry End, later known as the North Bank. At the same time the giant clock moved to the College End, which consequently became referred to as the Clock End.

The only significant changes until the 1980s were the reconstruction of the North Bank terrace roof after its bombing during the Second World War, the installation of floodlights in 1951, and that of undersoil heating in 1964. To the club's credit, even at the height of football hooliganism they refused

Building the terraces at the new ground in Highbury in 1913

to install perimeter fencing to prevent fans gaining access to the pitch, a move that ironically led to them not being awarded FA Cup semi-finals for a number of years.

In 1989, executive boxes were constructed above the Clock End terraces, giving partial cover to those

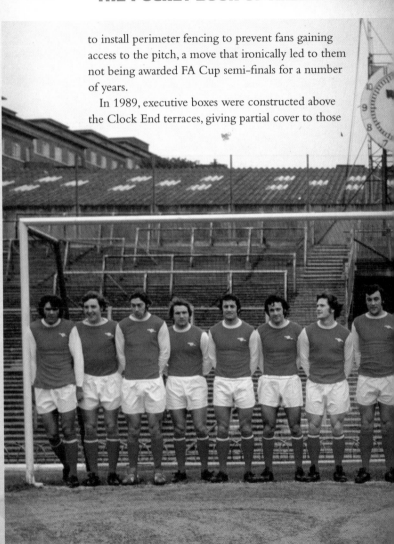

who stood below. However, the last major change
to the stadium was brought about by the post-
Hillsborough disaster recommendations of the Taylor
Report. Stadiums had to be converted to all seating,
so a new stand was built in place of the North Bank
terracing. It went up over the course of the 1992/93

The 1972 FA Cup final squad line up in front of the old Clock End

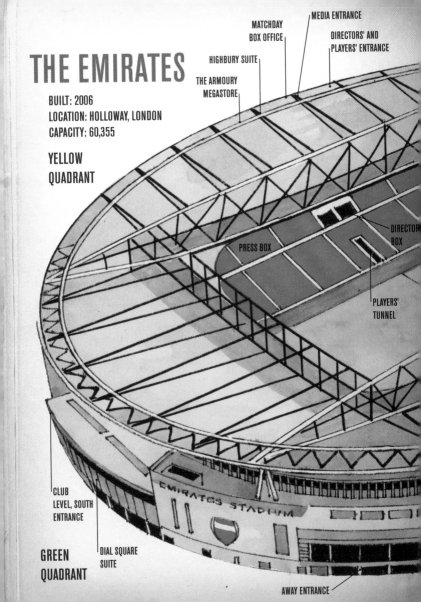

THE EMIRATES

BUILT: 2006
LOCATION: HOLLOWAY, LONDON
CAPACITY: 60,355

**YELLOW
QUADRANT**

MEDIA ENTRANCE

MATCHDAY
BOX OFFICE

DIRECTORS' AND
PLAYERS' ENTRANCE

HIGHBURY SUITE

THE ARMOURY
MEGASTORE

DIRECTOR
BOX

PRESS BOX

PLAYERS'
TUNNEL

CLUB
LEVEL, SOUTH
ENTRANCE

EMIRATES STADIUM

GREEN
QUADRANT

DIAL SQUARE
SUITE

AWAY ENTRANCE

ORANGE
QUADRANT

RED (SINGING)
SECTION

ROYAL
OAK SUITE

CLUB LEVEL,
NORTH ENTRANCE

EMIRATES STADIUM

BLUE
QUADRANT

WOOLWICH
SUITE

CLUB
LEVEL, EAST
ENTRANCE

season, the final time that standing was allowed at the
stadium, at the Clock End which was converted to
seating after the new stand opposite was completed.
The changes meant the capacity was reduced from
55,000 to 38,500, although the stadium's record
crowd of 73,295, for a match against Sunderland in

1935, was set in the days when there was less seating.

With the increased importance of corporate hospitality and the growing popularity of both Premiership football and Arsenal, it soon became apparent that, as in 1913, the club would have to move for financial reasons. When Arsène Wenger brought sustained success to the club, it became obvious it had outgrown its home. Hemmed in by residential housing on three sides, significant expansion was inconceivable, and so the directors looked at alternative locations for a new stadium.

They settled on a triangle of land housing light industrial premises and the local rubbish depot, a long goal-kick west of Highbury. The site became known as Ashburton Grove, after a road in the area. When the club received approval for its plans and raised the finance to build the new stadium, Highbury's days were numbered. The final season there was 2005/06, which culminated in a 4–2 victory over Wigan, securing Champions League football at the expense

The magnificent Art Deco facade of Highbury's East Stand

of neighbours Tottenham. It was a day that mixed exaltation with sadness. The stadium was subsequently developed into residential apartments, although the facades of the listed East and West Stands provide a permanent reminder of their previous use.

In financing their £420 million new home, the club struck a naming rights deal whereby it would be called 'The Emirates' for 15 years, promoting the eponymous middle eastern airline. Designed by HOK Sport, it was similar in look to the same company's Stadium of Light, the home of Lisbon's famous Benfica, although due to height restrictions the Emirates holds 5,000 fewer spectators, with a capacity of just over 60,000. The lower and upper tiers of the bowl-shaped stadium sandwich a middle ring that hosts 7,000 'club level' season ticket holders and 150 executive boxes. These premium-priced pews raise almost as much revenue per season as was made at Highbury from all spectators.

Supporters with memories of Arsenal's previous home bemoan the lack of atmosphere at the new ground, and many areas certainly suffer from a paucity of decoration, although the club intend to address this. Other differences from Highbury are that the pitch is much bigger and the fans are further from the playing surface. There is a perceived

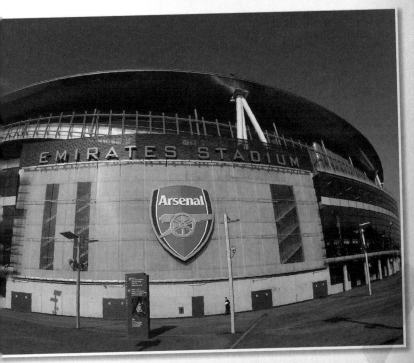

absence of the intimacy that was experienced before the move. However, it has been praised by football stadium expert Simon Inglis as "Britain's first truly 21st-century stadium". New memories have to be formed in the new surroundings to give fans more of a positive feeling about the place. In their first three seasons at the Emirates, Arsenal have failed to win a single major honour.

Opened in 2006, the Emirates cost £420m to build and, at 60,355, has the third highest capacity of a British football ground

GREAT GOALS

CHARLIE GEORGE
1971 FA CUP FINAL V LIVERPOOL

After a goalless 90 minutes the final came alive with a strike for each side in extra time, but with the sun mercilessly beating down it appeared as if a replay would be required to break the deadlock between the two teams.

Yet in the second period of extra time, despite looking visibly drained, Charlie George changed all that.

George Graham headed a Liverpool goal kick forward to John Radford who exchanged possession with George before teeing him up near the edge of the penalty area. "With his last ounce of energy," recalls coach Don Howe, "Charlie picks up the ball. He's about 25 yards out and I think 'He's going to have a go here'. It flew in."

George hit an unstoppable shot just inside Liverpool keeper Ray Clemence's post. The scorer himself says, "I was fortunate, I could strike a ball; 30 or 50 yards out, it didn't matter to me, I could always do that. As soon as it left my foot I knew it was a goal."

For his celebration, George laid on the Wembley turf with arms outstretched facing skywards. "He's lying on the floor, Charlie is," says Howe, "and he isn't celebrating, I'll tell you. He was well and truly knackered." Maybe so, but his work was done. Arsenal had won the 'double'.

LIAM BRADY
1978 FIRST DIVISION V TOTTENHAM

Christmas came early for Gooners in 1978. Two days before opening their presents, they enjoyed a five-goal win at the home of their bitter rivals, neighbours Tottenham.

The game is best remembered, despite an Alan Sunderland hat-trick, for Liam Brady's fourth goal.

As Spurs were attempting to clear their lines in the 66th minute, Brady dispossessed Peter Taylor. He had the option of passing to Frank Stapleton or using Graham Rix on his left, but with the game as good as won, he went for glory himself. He approached the edge of the Spurs box and then looped an exquisite curled shot into the keeper's top left hand corner.

BBC cameras were fortunately at the game and commentator John Motson exclaimed "Look at that. Oh, look at that," as the ball drifted into the net past the helpless Spurs defence, right in front of the ecstatic away section.

Brady's nickname was 'Chippy', although it was not derived from the technique he used to craft this goal, but rather his love of eating chips! The voting for the PFA player of the year happened soon after this match, and Brady's performance, capped off by his goal, may well have been the key factor in his winning the award when it was announced in the spring of the following year.

ALAN SUNDERLAND
1979 FA CUP FINAL V MANCHESTER UNITED

Arsenal seemed to be counting down the clock to their first trophy in eight years at 2-0 up as the final entered the final five minutes of normal time. But a pair of quick goals from Manchester United took the wind out of Arsenal's sails and silenced the Gunners' crowd. Captain Pat Rice admits, "If the game had gone into extra time I honestly believe they would have beaten us. We were on a real downer, 2-0 up, coasting it... and all of a sudden bang, bang. We were really choked."

With a minute to go, Arsenal restarted the game after the equaliser. The ball came to Liam Brady just inside the opposition half and he began to dribble in the direction of the penalty area. He recalls, "I just wanted to get the ball in their half because I thought United were likely to score again." He slipped the ball wide to the left touchline and Graham Rix, whose pinpoint cross went over keeper Gary Bailey at the near post and fell invitingly for the onrushing Alan Sunderland. He slid the ball home past lunging defender Arthur Albiston.

From happiness to concern to depression to ecstacy – all within the space of five minutes. The goal concluded a rollercoaster of emotions for all involved both on and off the pitch.

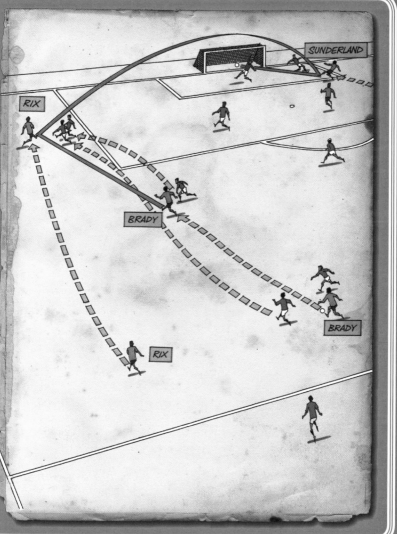

IAN WRIGHT
1993 PREMIERSHIP
V EVERTON

In the latter years of the George Graham era, Arsenal often resorted to getting the ball to Ian Wright as quickly as possible as their best method of scoring goals.

Purists didn't approve, although the fans enjoyed the cup successes that prioritising the defence brought about. The approach helped Wright eventually become the leading goalscorer in the club's history, scoring many memorable goals in the process.

This one against Everton was one of his best, from an early season 2-0 Premiership victory at Highbury in which Wright netted both goals. It showed the player had a deft touch to go with his chief weapon of pace.

Gunners' keeper David Seaman launched a long clearance and the ball sailed over Kevin Campbell before bouncing into the path of Wright, who controlled it with some keepy uppy, switching it from his right to his left, dinking it into the area and leaving his hapless marker not knowing which way to turn.

Wright describes it as "my all time best goal." He remembers, "My first intention was not to do what I did in the end, but the momentum of everything took me one way, then the other, and then the ball just bounced nicely as the defender was coming to try and tackle me. And I just lifted it over Neville Southall."

TONY ADAMS
1998 PREMIERSHIP
V EVERTON

Arsenal, with three Premiership matches remaining, needed to beat Everton at Highbury to celebrate their first title under Arsène Wenger in front of their home crowd.

By the time Tony Adams joined those on the scoresheet, the ephemera required for a trophy presentation was being prepared at the side of the North Bank, with the team 3-0 up.

Wenger brought on centre back Steve Bould for striker Christopher Wreh with ten minutes remaining. He took up a position in central midfield and, surprisingly, didn't look out of place. David Platt blocked an Everton move just inside his own half and the ball fell to Bould. Sensing the opportunity to break, Adams sprinted past. Bould took a couple of touches to allow his captain time to move forward, before he played a delicate chip over the advancing Everton defence. Wenger said, "I call Steve 'The Kaiser'" – after Franz Beckenbauer. His pass was worthy of the German great.

The attempt to play the offside trap failed, leaving Adams free to control the ball by knocking it down with his midriff. He says of the goal, "Although I pushed it onto my weaker left foot, the touch with my stomach was just good enough. I swung at it and the next thing I knew the net was bulging. It was a beautiful moment."

ADAMS

BOULD

ADAMS

PLATT

DENNIS BERGKAMP
2002 PREMIERSHIP V NEWCASTLE

With 28 matches of the Premiership season played, Arsenal travelled to St James' Park level on points with Manchester United at the top of the table. Newcastle were only two points behind in fourth place. A wonder goal after 25 minutes from Dennis Bergkamp was the first in a vital 2-0 victory. Patrick Vieira won the ball and gave it to Bergkamp, deep in Arsenal's half. He hit a crossfield ball to the advancing Robert Pires, who carried it forward on the left. Meanwhile, Bergkamp made a lung-busting run towards the Newcastle area. Pires spotted him and played the ball in to his feet.

Bergkamp described the pass as being "a little bit behind me." Tightly marked by Newcastle defender Nikos Dabizas, and facing away from the goal, he took one touch with his right foot to send the ball to the defender's right, whilst spinning to run past a bemused Dabizas on his other side. He effectively collected his own pass on the goal-side of the beaten defender, and had just enough time to re-adjust his body so he could slot it home with his favoured right foot. Bergkamp explained, "It looked quite a special move but it was the most effective way. When it works out it's fantastic, but if it doesn't people would wonder why I did it."

THIERRY HENRY
2002 PREMIERSHIP V TOTTENHAM

Goals against Tottenham have an extra significance for Arsenal fans. Thierry Henry's opener in this 3-0 derby victory was even more special for both the manner of the goal and its celebration.

In the 14th minute, Henry picked up a headed Patrick Vieira clearance and began a run towards the Spurs half. Closely shadowed by Matthew Etherington, his speed ended his marker's attentions as he honed in on Spurs' box. With defenders still to beat, he carried the ball across the edge of the area to set himself up for a left foot shot that beat the keeper at his near post.

BBC Radio Football Correspondent Mike Ingham summarised it thus: "Back defending initially, capturing possession, close control, pace, desire, tunnel vision, all opposition left trailing, three quarters of the length of Highbury covered, Kasey Keller helpless, North Bank End, 1-0. If that's not goal of the season, I'm looking forward to seeing the winner."

After scoring, Henry ran the length of the pitch to come to a halt on his knees in front of the away section. Encapsulating the significance of a north London derby strike, he reflected, "The goal was a good goal... especially against Tottenham." As for the celebration, "I don't know why I ran so far after the goal. I was dead for nearly two days after that."

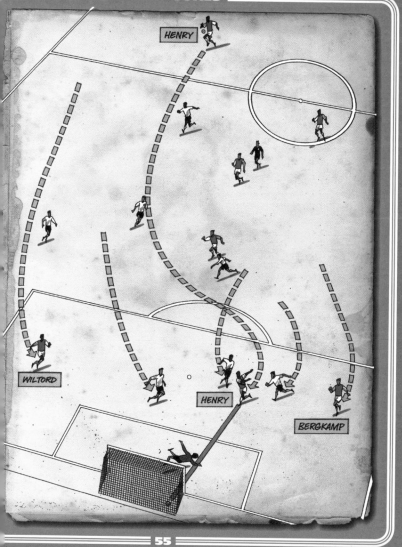

HENRY

HENRY

WILTORD

HENRY

BERGKAMP

WINNING ON ENEMY TURF

Arsenal have a unique record of winning league titles at the homes of their most intense rivals – those closest to them geographically or in the league table. It is as much of a quirk of the fixture list as anything else, as the two sides that have won more titles – Liverpool and Manchester United – have no such experiences. In 1933 and 1934, Arsenal won the title at Chelsea's Stamford Bridge. Here's the story of four of the instances in which the Gunners have landed titles at the stadiums where success tasted sweetest.

Bob Wilson jumps for joy as Arsenal clinch the 1971 double at the home of neighbours Tottenham Hotspur

v Tottenham, White Hart Lane, Monday 3rd May 1971

It was the lock out of all lock outs, with 51,000 inside and 100,000 unable to gain access. Arsenal were going for the league championship and FA Cup double, and this, their final First Division fixture of the season, was the first trophy to be resolved. The majority of the crowd were Arsenal fans, so the atmosphere was akin to a home game. To pip Leeds United to first place, Arsenal needed either a goalless draw or a win. So when Ray Kennedy put the team 1-0 up in the 87th minute, the title was by no means secured. "That was the longest three minutes I have ever known," Kennedy later said of the period after the goal when the home side did their utmost to poop the party.

v Liverpool, Anfield, Friday 26th May 1989

Due to the Hillsborough disaster, this fixture was played almost a fortnight after the league programme should have been completed. Leaders Liverpool hosted

Adams, Hayes, Rocastle and Merson celebrate snatching the title on an unforgettable night of drama at Anfield in 1989

second-placed Arsenal in what had become a title decider. Although George Graham's team had dropped five points in their previous two matches, what is rarely remembered is that even if they had won both games, Liverpool could still have won the title by a point simply by beating the Gunners at home.

As it was, a two-goal win was required by Arsenal, but the underdogs achieved the required result, scoring twice without reply with Michael Thomas's late goal providing the most dramatic conclusion to a league season in living memory.

v Manchester United, Old Trafford, Wednesday 8th May 2002

In a reverse of the circumstances of 1971, Arsenal were attempting to win another double by claiming the Premiership title after winning the FA Cup final. Arsène Wenger's team were five points clear of United, with two matches to play. Their hosts had to win this game and hope that Arsenal might fail to beat Everton the following weekend to have any chance of overtaking them.

On paper United's chances looked to be improved by the absence of key

men Adams, Henry, Bergkamp and Pires. However,
it turned out to be a 90 minutes Arsenal largely
controlled, sealing the title with the only goal of the
game from Sylvain Wiltord after 56 minutes.

A banner in the away corner at full time said it all –
'Champions' Section'.

v Tottenham, White Hart Lane, Sunday 25th April 2004

When news
filtered through
before kick off that
nearest challengers
Chelsea had
been defeated
by Newcastle,
Arsenal's task was clear. Avoid defeat at Spurs and
they would win the title with four matches to spare.

They started by playing football of the order that had
seen them reach this stage of the campaign without
suffering a solitary league defeat, with collectors' item
goals from Vieira and Pires in the first half.

The Gunners were cruising, but took it a little too
easy and allowed Spurs back into the game. A late
equaliser gave the home fans a smidgen of pride,
but the afternoon – and once more the home of
their local rivals – belonged to the newly-crowned
champions of England.

ARSENAL COMIC STRIP HISTORY 2

AFTER A 1970 FAIRS CUP MATCH IN ROME AGAINST LAZIO, THE PLAYERS OF BOTH TEAMS WERE INVITED TO A RESTAURANT WHERE THE VISITING PLAYERS WERE PRESENTED WITH LEATHER BAGS ...

OOOOH... THAT'S NICE...

THE ARSENAL LADS STARTED THROWING THEM AROUND, AND BEFORE LONG A LAZIO PLAYER WAS HIT BY ONE, AND RETURNED IT WITH INTEREST TO BOB McNAB!

A MASS BRAWL BROKE OUT— 'LIKE THE WILD WEST' REMEMBERS FRANK McLINTOCK ...

AFTER THIS INCIDENCE OF 'HANDBAGS' UEFA BANNED POST-MATCH SOCIALIZING BETWEEN TEAMS!

THE STORY OF THE GUNNERS
RISE AND FALL
1925-65

At the same time as Herbert Chapman agreed to become Arsenal's manager, the rules of the game were evolving, and a modification to the offside rule meant goals became easier to score.

Something had to be done to reduce the number the defence was conceding, and it meant changes for both Arsenal's formation and their fortunes as the new boss set to work. After a 7-0 loss to Newcastle in October 1925 a team meeting was held by the manager, with the formation changing from 2-3-5 to 3-2-5 (or 3-4-3) as a result. It was effected by playing the centre half closer to his own goal, between the two full backs, and became known as the "WM" formation. Immediately, the team's results improved as they finished the first season under Chapman as First Division runners up, behind his old side Huddersfield.

However, chairman Henry Norris refused to allow his manager to spend enough money to strengthen his team, and the following season they fell away, finishing 11th. The conservatism of the club at boardroom level when it came to big money signings was to become a frequent phenomenon in Arsenal's history. The FA Cup provided some consolation, as the team made it to their first final in the competition, even if it was a disappointing day at Wembley, Arsenal losing 1-0 to Cardiff when a freak goal saw keeper Dan Lewis bundle the ball into his own net. Forward Charlie Buchan described the moment: "Lewis gathered the ball in his arms.

As he rose, his knee hit the ball and sent it out of his grasp. In trying to retrieve it, he only knocked it further towards the goal. The ball trickled slowly but inexorably over the goal-line with hardly enough strength to reach the net."

There may have been suspicions about the methods of persuasion exercised by Henry Norris to ensure Arsenal's place in the First Division after the war, but more concrete evidence of under-the-counter payments to persuade Charlie Buchan to join the club from Sunderland in 1925 eventually surfaced and the chairman was banned from football for life.

Captain Charlie Buchan leads the Gunners out at Highbury for the opening game of the 1925 season

Samuel Hill-Wood succeeded Norris as chairman and both his son Denis and grandson Peter later served in the role. Chapman was given money to spend and bought the best players available to build a team that would dominate the 1930s. The moniker of 'the Bank of England' club came from this time, although future generations were to equate the idea with financial conservatism rather than having pots of money.

Arsenal's first trophy in a decade of glory was the 1930 FA Cup. A year later, they became the first southern club to win the First Division title. A second followed two seasons later when Chapman introduced white sleeves to Arsenal's red shirts, a look that has become so familiar today. The 1933 title was the first of three in a row, although Chapman tragically died of pneumonia in January 1934 so was unable to see the team he had built win a further three titles and another FA Cup before the onset of the Second World War. George Allison, also the managing director, was appointed manager to replace the departed Chapman, although he delegated the running of the team to two of his existing staff – one of whom was future manager Tom Whittaker – for the rest of the 1933/34 season.

Allison continued Chapman's work of buying players who would improve the team, with Ted Drake arriving from Southampton only two months after Chapman's death. It was an inspired buy, as his 42 goals in 41 league games helped secure another title

The Graf Zeppelin looms over Wembley as Arsenal play Huddersfield in the 1930 FA Cup final

in his first full season at the club, before he netted a
club record seven in one game away to Aston Villa in
December 1935. Arsenal's failure to win the title for
a fourth time on the trot in 1936 was largely down
to Drake missing ten weeks through a knee injury,
although he returned in time to help win the FA
Cup. After a fifth championship in eight seasons in

1938, only one more campaign would be completed before the onset of the Second World War, which saw eight of the club's players lose their lives on active duty.

When football recommenced, a disappointing 13th place finish in the 1946/47 table was followed by George Allison's resignation. His task was not

From left: Wilf Copping, Eddie Hapgood, George Male, Ted Drake and Cliff Bastin in 1935

helped by the retirement of some of the
players who had been so instrumental in the
pre-war success, and of course the absence
of those who had died in the war. Tom
Whittaker stepped up from his position as
first team trainer to become Arsenal's third
great manager in succession. His influence was
immediate and the 1948 title was landed in
his first season at the helm. The club remained
consistent competitors under Whittaker and
made the FA Cup final in both 1950 (which
they won against Liverpool) and 1952 (a defeat
to Newcastle). Another league title was won
in 1953.

However, Arsenal fans would have a long
wait to see more silverware. The team began
to decline and despite the occasional star such
as Joe Baker and George Eastham, the trophies
that were won by London teams were enjoyed
by Tottenham, Chelsea and West Ham. Since
the arrival of Herbert Chapman, Gunners'
fans had never endured such lean times. Tom
Whittaker died of a heart attack in 1956 and
the managers that followed – Jack Crayston,
George Swindin (1958) and Billy Wright (1962) –
failed to bring back the good times, despite no one
team dominating the 1950s and 60s. The lowpoint
of this period was the attendance for a home match
against Leeds United in May 1966. Whether Arsenal's
3-0 defeat or the attendance figure of a mere 4,554

spectators was more humiliating is a moot point, but manager Billy Wright was dismissed weeks later.

His successor was found amongst the existing staff at the club. Physiotherapist Bertie Mee was promoted to attempt to revive Arsenal's fortunes.

Captain Joe Mercer clutches the FA Cup after the 1950 final win

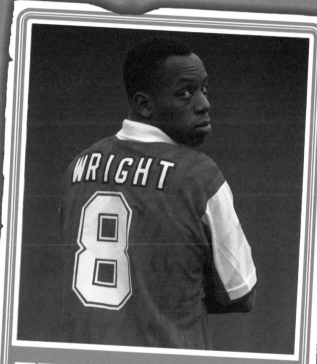

TRUE COLOURS
THE HISTORY OF THE KIT

The original Dial Square/
Royal Arsenal kit of 1886

Arsenal's humble origins meant
that for the club's very first matches, players
provided their own kits, and the colours
they sported did not match.

This situation only lasted until one of the
players, Fred Beardsley, wrote to his old club
Nottingham Forest to ask if they could help with
some spare kit. He had relocated south for
work, but with football more established
in the north, Forest were able to donate a
complete set of dark red shirts and so the
development of Arsenal's kit began.

The long-sleeved shirts featured a
collar and buttons down the front. They
were paired with knee-length white shorts
and heavy woollen red socks. This colour
scheme for the shirts and shorts remained
until the early 1930s (although sometimes
socks changed from red to navy blue).
Occasionally a club crest was sewn on the
shirt for high profile matches, but there were
no major changes, aside from the shade of red
becoming lighter and the sometime use of a
lace-up collar.

Manager Herbert Chapman, always considering
innovations that would give his players an
advantage, introduced hooped socks in 1932,
reasoning it would help the players
distinguish their team-mates more quickly.

But as far as the long-term future of Arsenal's kit was concerned, a far more significant change was to follow the next year.

Herbert Chapman introduced the white sleeves in 1933

There are two versions of how Chapman came about the idea of introducing white sleeves to the shirt. One has him playing golf with Tom Webster, a famous cartoonist of the time, who was wearing a red sleeveless sweater over a white shirt. The other has the Gunners' manager spotting someone at the ground wearing similar attire. Whichever is true, he was struck by how the combination stood out, and the red shirt with white sleeves was adopted. The kit remained as red shirt with white collar and sleeves, white shorts and hooped blue and white socks for over 20 years.

Other changes were gradual. In 1938, a few years after Chapman's death, the authorities saw the sense in his idea of numbers on the back of shirts to help identify the players. The white collar was replaced with a simple v-neck cut in the late 1950s, when lighter cotton jerseys were introduced.

Arsenal's change colours for their first

The 1950 FA Cup final gold change shirt was worn only once

few decades tended to be white shirts with black shorts. But one of the most famous away strips was that worn for the 1950 FA Cup final against Liverpool. As the two finalists wore red for their first choice kits, it was decided that both should change and manager Tom Whittaker came up with the idea for gold coloured shirts. Images of winning captain Joe Mercer with the trophy have helped give this shirt an almost mystical status, in spite of it only being worn for this match. In fact, Arsenal reverted to away kits dominated by either white or blue until the late 1960s.

The home shirt, by this time having returned to a collarless round neck, underwent a radical change between 1965 and 1967, when the white sleeves were abandoned. The attendant lack of success in this era may have been an unhappy coincidence, but when the white sleeves returned, fortunes improved. In the late 1960s a cannon logo was added to the chest, and this version of the kit, sported in the 1971 double season and the remainder of the 1970s (before the introduction of shirt

sponsors and bi-annual design changes) is regarded as
the classic version of the strip by most fans today. In
tandem, Arsenal settled on yellow shirts and
socks with blue shorts for their away colours,
and despite only being utilised since 1969, the
combination has come to be regarded by
purists as that in which all Arsenal sides
should play if a change strip is
necessary.

The 1980s saw changes
begin to occur more rapidly.
Apart from the introduction
of a shirt sponsor (JVC) in
1981, the kit manufacturers
(Umbro) began to feature their
own logo. The replica kit market
was steadily growing as fans were
able to buy the shirts, which in turn
fuelled more changes. Today, there are
two new kits for supporters to buy
each summer. Even though the home
top is changed every two years, the
proliferation of change strips means
that kits are released which may only
be worn a few times by the team, yet
the profits they garner mean a big
push to sell them by the club. In turn,
this has led to competition between
kit manufacturers for the contract
to produce Arsenal's strip, with

The classic 1970s
home strip

Adidas taking over from 1986 until 1994, and Nike ever since. The sponsors changed to Dreamcast (in 1999), then O2 (2002), and since the 2006 stadium move, the Emirates airline.

As for the away shirts, the policy of continually producing different kits has led to some unusual results. In 1982, the change strip consisted of a green shirt with navy blue sleeves and shorts, whilst the socks were hooped affairs combining the two colours.

Purists favour the simple away strip introduced in 1969…

Another unusual version was the 'tractor tyre' variation on yellow and blue produced in 1991. It was such an eyesore that spectators could be forgiven for wearing sunglasses to watch the team play, although that season did mark the cannon emblem being replaced by the full club crest.

Amongst the different colours the change strips have featured since have been blue, gold, white, maroon and navy blue hoops, and good old yellow.

For the 1993 League Cup final, squad numbers

were utilised rather than the traditional numbering of a starting eleven. Additionally, the players' names were printed above their number. This innovation was also used for the FA Cup final and introduced across the Premier League the following August.

Highbury's final season saw the team wear a maroon (labelled 'redcurrant' for marketing purposes) and white home kit commemorating that worn in their first season there in 1913. With this exception, despite suffering a redesign every other year, the home top has remained true to the basic idea of a red shirt with white sleeves, albeit in the current 2009 version with the amount of white on the sleeve being little more than a white strip. One Arsenal kit tradition that never changes is that the captain decides whether the team will wear short or long-sleeved shirts for each match.

... a marked contrast with the infamous 1991 'tractor tyre' design

HALL OF FAME

TONY ADAMS

Tony Adams was Arsenal's most successful ever captain, leading the club to nine trophies over the course of three different decades.

Incredibly, before 1996, he did so in spite of the handicap of alcohol addiction, which even led to a spell in prison (after he was convicted of driving over the limit) during his second title-winning season.

An obviously talented central defender, he had all the necessary attributes from a young age to skipper the club. Even so, it came as a surprise when George Graham, following a dispute with the existing captain Kenny Sansom, handed Adams the armband at the age of 21.

It turned out to be an inspired move, as Adams proved so adept at the role he fulfilled it for three different managers.

A glut of trophies soon followed, prompted by Adams's abilities as both a defender and an organiser of others. "I've never had a problem with confidence," he revealed. It was a mindset that led him to inspire his colleagues to against-the-odds trophy-winning triumphs such as the victories at Liverpool in 1989 and against Parma five years later.

He was also chosen as skipper of England under several managers.

Arsène Wenger's arrival in 1996 gave him a new lease of life at the same time as he renounced drink. The new manager's insistence that his defenders pass the ball out rather than hoof it clear revealed Adams was more than simply a battering ram.

"I always believed I was a bloody good footballer," he said in 1997. "Now I'm playing without fear."

Added to the fresh approach to the physical preparation of players, it extended Adams's career long enough for him to inspire the Gunners to a pair of league and cup doubles before the man George Graham dubbed "a colossus" called it a day in May 2002. He was the definitive one-club man, although ultimately that proved to be thanks to Wenger.

"He's a pure joy to work for," enthused Adams in 2000. "I play for him now, and if I didn't have him I wouldn't be at Arsenal."

> **" The Arsenal back four were all university graduates in the art of defending. I consider Tony Adams to be a professor of defence. He is simply outstanding "**
> Arsène Wenger

TONY ADAMS FACTFILE

Born: Romford, Essex, 10th October 1966

Arsenal appearances: 669

Arsenal goals: 48

Honours won with Arsenal: League Championship (1989, 1991), Premiership (1998, 2002), European Cup Winners' Cup (1994), FA Cup (1993, 1998, 2002), League Cup (1987, 1993)

Other clubs: None

International appearances: England, 66 caps, 5 goals

CLIFF BASTIN

Cliff Bastin only appeared for his local club Exeter for one season, during which he was spotted by Herbert Chapman and brought to Arsenal, aged 17, in 1929.

Given the nickname 'Boy Bastin' for obvious reasons, he demonstrated coolness and accuracy in front of goal, assets he would utilise when he became the team's penalty taker.

Played mostly as a left winger at Arsenal, one of the reasons he was a prolific scorer was Chapman's instruction that wide players were to cut in rather than hug the wings, and the supply of chances forged by the play of Alex James ensured Bastin enjoyed plenty of opportunities. He frequently took a position ten yards in from the touchline, cognisant of what James was likely to do.

Bastin played a part in all of the trophies won by the club during the 1930s, going on to become Arsenal's record goalscorer, a distinction he held for 58 years until Ian Wright finally overtook his tally in 1997. He also enjoyed international success with England during the 1930s, making his debut at the age of 19.

After finishing top scorer for his club in 1932/33 and 1933/34, Bastin was usurped in the goals scored table when Ted Drake arrived at Arsenal.

Bastin was played in other positions in seasons the team failed to win the league. When he was moved back to his favoured position in 1937/38, Arsenal won the title again, in no small part thanks to the increase in Bastin's goal tally.

Injury to his right leg meant he was absent for much of the following season, before the war interrupted his career at a time (aged 27) he should have been reaching his peak.

Bastin's increasing deafness meant he was excused military service, and so he served in the war as an air raid warden, ironically stationed at the top of the Highbury Stadium with future Arsenal manager Tom Whittaker. He played wartime football (making around 250 appearances) to keep up the morale of civilians, yet his leg never fully recovered and after the war he played only seven more times for the club, before retiring in 1947 and returning to Exeter to run a pub.

> **ff Cliff Bastin had a trait few of us are blessed with, an ice-cold nerve JJ**
> Tom Whittaker

Born: **Exeter, Devon, 14th March 1912**

Arsenal appearances: **396**

Arsenal goals: **178**

Honours won with Arsenal: **League Championship (1931, 1933, 1934, 1935, 1938), FA Cup (1930, 1936)**

Other clubs: **Exeter City (1928)**

International appearances: **England 21 caps, 12 goals**

CLIFF BASTIN FACTFILE

DENNIS BERGKAMP

Dennis Bergkamp's signing in 1995 signified the moment that Arsenal declared their ambitions to become one of the top teams in world football.

He was the kind of undisputed international superstar who excites supporters into a frenzy before he has even kicked a ball. Although the player had not enjoyed a happy time while at Inter Milan, his reputation as a visionary who made the game look easy remained undiminished when he arrived in north London.

He played as a shadow striker behind an out and out forward, initially Ian Wright, then Nicolas Anelka and finally Thierry Henry. His tactical awareness and deft passes meant he was ideally suited to play 'in the hole'. From there, he scored some memorable goals and set up countless others.

As he became settled, the team's league position improved. Fifth in his first season, third in his second (after

Wenger's arrival) and champions in 1997/98, when he also won both the Footballer of the Year and Players' Player awards.

At the beginning of that season, Wenger said: "Can you say Bergkamp is not the best player in the world right now? If there is better, I have not seen him." Gooners simply called him 'God'.

His presence was vital in attracting others to the club. He reflected after the first Premiership title, "I was part of the start and then the boss came, Vieira, Petit, Overmars and then on to this team where they're basically all world-class players. Maybe 15 years ago they wouldn't have played for Arsenal, but they do now and I helped that."

If he was like a magnet to other players, it was nothing compared to his effect on the fans. He was big box office, as 'Sold Out' signs became the order of the day.

In spite of his playing well into his thirties, he remained a key man in the five trophy victories between 2002 and 2005, before bowing out at the end of Highbury's final season.

That it was his testimonial game which opened the new stadium proved a fitting tribute to an Arsenal legend.

❝ Dennis is the best player I have ever played with as a partner. It is a dream for a striker to have him in the team with you ❞
Thierry Henry

Born: **Amsterdam, Holland, 10th May 1969**

Arsenal appearances: 424

Arsenal goals: 120

Honours won with Arsenal: **Premiership (1998, 2002, 2004), FA Cup (2002, 2003, 2005)**

Other clubs: Ajax (1986), Inter Milan (1993)

International appearances: Holland, 79 caps, 37 goals

DENNIS BERGKAMP FACTFILE

LIAM BRADY

Liam Brady was a midfield maestro who lit up the Gunners in a period of relative gloom – the mid to late 1970s.

He came into the side during a period when Arsenal flirted with relegation. However, the arrival of Terry Neill as manager and the return of Don Howe as coach improved things as Brady's game itself developed, with the club reaching four cup finals over three seasons from 1978 to 1980. The Irishman possessed an abundance of skill and was an adept reader of the game. Despite his relatively scrawny physique, he was deceptively strong and difficult to dispossess, especially when dribbling through opponents.

Pat Rice, captain during the latter part of Brady's Arsenal career, remembers, "The lower half of his body was so strong he just ghosted past people." And he had such a quick brain that he could either play people in, play one-twos, float a ball in or score tremendous goals himself. Indeed, as well as enjoying the ability to set up team-mates, Brady's sweet left foot ensured 'Chippy', as he was nicknamed, chipped in with his share of goals. His talent for striking a ball with minimal backlift often made it difficult for rivals to predict his intentions before he released the ball.

> **There was never any doubt he would be a great because not only did he want to be a fine player, he wanted to win**
> Don Howe

Yet only one of the four cup finals he played in ended in victory, the 1979 FA Cup won thanks to a last-minute goal against Manchester United. Brady played a key part in the creation of all three Arsenal strikes that afternoon. The same season he was awarded the PFA Players' Player of the Year award.

But as the leading light in a team that never looked like seriously challenging for the league title, he grew frustrated and the club agreed to let him go in 1980.

He moved to Italian giants Juventus, whom he had performed against so admirably in the victorious European Cup Winners' Cup semi-final. Unfortunately, Brady could not give Arsenal fans a happy ending to his time at Highbury, missing a penalty in the shoot-out against Valencia in the subsequent final.

Born: Dublin, 13th February 1956

Arsenal appearances: 306

Arsenal goals: 59

Honours won with Arsenal: FA Cup (1979)

Other clubs: Juventus (1980), Sampdoria (1982), Inter Milan (1984), Ascoli (1986), West Ham (1987)

International appearances: Republic of Ireland, 72 caps, 9 goals

LIAM BRADY FACTFILE

THIERRY HENRY

Nicolas Anelka's 1999 move to Real Madrid netted a £22 million fee which paid for Arsenal's state of the art training centre and a certain Thierry Henry.

Arsène Wenger quickly set about transforming the speedy winger into a centre forward, and by the time he left for Barcelona eight years later, Henry had been voted the greatest ever Gunner in a club website poll of supporters.

He played the game with power, pace, precision and at times, total freedom of expression, making him almost impossible to shackle. As Everton boss David Moyes succinctly put it, "Henry occupies all the players at the back on his own."

He was surrounded by the talents of superstar team-mates and, if anything, the five trophies in four seasons from 2002 were an underachievement from a team that was unquestionably the best in England at the time. Over this period, despite never actually winning any of the various individual prizes for a specific season, many neutrals believed Henry to be the best player in world football. The sight of the number 14 being applauded off the pitch by opposition fans when the Gunners played away was not unusual.

> **He'll go down in the history not only of Arsenal but of football**
> Arsène Wenger

After Patrick Vieira's departure, he was made club captain for the final season at Highbury (scoring the last ever goal there) and the first campaign at the Emirates. In October 2005 away to Sparta Prague he converted twice to replace Ian Wright as the club's all-time record goalscorer. His goals were rarely mundane, sometimes almost works of art.

Henry encapsulated the perfect footballer for the manager, combining his multifarious abilities with the right attitude. The striker said of his approach, "When I am on the pitch, I will give it 100 per cent. You can never doubt my commitment. I play with my heart."

In his initial season as skipper he led the team to their first ever Champions League final, where he gallantly attempted to win the game for ten man Arsenal as a lone striker in a performance that was all about character.

Born: **Les Ulis, Essonne, France, 17th August 1977**
Arsenal appearances: **370**
Arsenal goals: **226**
Honours won with Arsenal:
Premiership (2002, 2004), FA Cup (2002, 2003, 2005)
Other clubs: **Monaco (1994), Juventus (1999), Barcelona (2007)**
International appearances:
France, 111 caps, 48 goals

THIERRY HENRY FACTFILE

ALEX JAMES

Herbert Chapman signed inside forward James from Second Division Preston in 1929.

The previous year, he had come to the attention of leading clubs due to a brace of goals as Scotland's famous 'Wembley Wizards' demolished England 5-1 at the stadium.

The maximum wage, set by the Football League at the time, was £8 a week but the player was unhappy with this at Preston, not least because other clubs had found a way round the rule. So Arsenal arranged for leading department store Selfridges to employ him as a 'sports demonstrator' for £250 a year.

On the field, he had to adapt to a deeper role at Highbury, playing as a link man to create chances for others in the 3-4-3 system that Chapman was honing. He found it difficult initially and was dropped from the starting line-up.

He returned in time for the 1930 FA Cup final and his contribution was key. For the opening goal in the 2-0 victory over Huddersfield, he took a quick free kick, executing a one-two with Cliff Bastin before rocketing the ball into the net against an unprepared defence.

"It was one of the smartest moves ever made in a big match and it gave us the Cup," said team-mate Eddie Hapgood.

Arsenal won four titles between 1931 and 1935, and it was no coincidence that the one time they narrowly missed out (in 1932) James missed the run-in due to a serious knee ligament injury. His value to the team in his deep creative position was summed up by Matt Busby, then a player with Manchester City. "The number of goals created from rearguard beginnings by Alex James were the most significant factor in Arsenal's greatness," said Busby.

His trademark look was baggy shorts – sported to hide the long johns he wore to keep warm (he suffered from rheumatism) – and a distinctive heavily-gelled centre parting. He captained the side to the final honour he would win with the club, the 1936 FA Cup, beating Sheffield United.

A year later he retired, arguably the most important player in Arsenal's dominance of the decade.

> ❝ Alex James was widely regarded as the most astute football tactician of his time ❞
>
> Stanley Matthews

Born: Mossend, Lanarkshire, 14th September 1901

Arsenal appearances: 261

Arsenal goals: 27

Honours won with Arsenal:
League Championship (1931, 1933, 1934, 1935), FA Cup (1930, 1936)

Other clubs: Raith Rovers (1922), Preston North End (1927)

International appearances:
Scotland, 8 caps, 3 goals

ALEX JAMES FACTFILE

JOE MERCER

Joe Mercer was brought from Everton in November 1946 at a time when Arsenal were languishing in 21st place in the First Division table.

His arrival transformed the team and he was made temporary captain at the start of his first full season. When club captain Leslie Compton returned from his cricketing duties after the Gunners had made a blazing start, he insisted Mercer remain skipper. They went on to secure the league championship, with Mercer's experience of winning the title with Everton in 1939 undoubtedly a key asset.

Although an attack-minded left half at his previous club, he was converted to a more defensive role at Highbury. However, his domestic circumstances remained unaltered, as he was allowed to live and train on Merseyside, only joining up with his team-mates on matchdays.

In 1950, he led the team to a successful FA Cup final against Liverpool, and was voted Footballer of the Year that season. Although a second FA Cup final appearance – against Newcastle – two years later ended in disappointment, a second title under his captaincy followed in 1953.

Fellow post-war great Len Shackleton believed "Joe Mercer, as an Arsenal player between his 30th and 40th birthdays, was a far better wing half than in his younger days. When he discovered his legs would not allow him to run all over the field, and played almost entirely in his own half, he was great. The service of wonderful passes that flowed from this spindly bow-legged genius was, I am certain, 50 per cent of the reason for Arsenal's post-war successes."

His ability to intercept and distribute was key, in tandem with his shrewd tactical knowledge and a talent to inspire confidence in his team-mates.

Mercer decided to retire in May 1953, but changed his mind and returned to the game, lining up to help Arsenal as they tried to defend their title.

However, in April the following year he had no option but to call time on his playing career, suffering a broken leg after colliding with a colleague in a match against Liverpool.

> **Joe Mercer was a tremendous tackler, timing his interventions perfectly. He had a deceptive speed**
> Tommy Lawton

Born: Ellesmere Port, Cheshire, 9th August 1914
Arsenal appearances: 275
Arsenal goals: 2
Honours won with Arsenal: League Championship (1948, 1953), FA Cup (1950)
Other clubs: Everton (1932)
International appearances: England, 5 caps, 0 goals

JOE MERCER FACTFILE

FRANK McLINTOCK

Frank McLintock was one of a number of great Arsenal captains. He joined the club from Leicester City in 1964, and was made skipper in 1967.

A natural for the job, he recalls, "I was very good at sorting people out, pushing them around, exaggerating praise for people. It never entered my head that I shouldn't tell someone what they should be doing."

The Gunners were in the process of transformation, and success beckoned with two consecutive League Cup final appearances at the end of the Sixties. However, after winning neither (making him a four-time Wembley cup final loser), the disheartened captain handed in a transfer request.

Coach Don Howe persuaded McLintock to remain, and had the idea of converting him from central midfield to the heart of the defence the following season. Despite his relative lack of height for the position, it proved an inspired switch. He demonstrated an excellent reading of the game and a cool head, without losing the infectious passion that at times in midfield meant he tried to do too much.

A first trophy in 18 seasons followed, as Arsenal won the Fairs Cup, in no small part thanks to the captain's rousing of his players after the final first leg defeat away to Anderlecht.

But better was to come in 1970/71 with honours for both man and club as he led the Gunners to the League Championship and FA Cup double and took the Footballer of the Year award.

The experience of losing his first four finals at Wembley meant he refused to let the opportunity to win one go easily, and once again he rallied his troops when Liverpool took an extra time lead in the 1971 FA Cup final. "Come on, we can still win it!" he roared, as the final 2-1 scoreline to Arsenal confirmed.

Despite narrowly failing to successfully defend either trophy in 1972, manager Bertie Mee allowed McLintock to leave the club for Queens Park Rangers a year later. It was a mistake that signaled the end of a golden Gunners era.

> **He was a great leader, an inspiration. He could pick everybody up or give them a rollicking when they needed it**
> Jon Sammels

Born: Glasgow, 28th December 1939

Arsenal appearances: 403

Arsenal goals: 32

Honours won with Arsenal: European Inter-Cities Fairs Cup (1970), League Championship (1971), FA Cup (1971)

Other clubs: Leicester City (1957), Queens Park Rangers (1973)

International appearances: Scotland, 9 caps, 1 goal

FRANK McLINTOCK FACTFILE

PATRICK VIEIRA

The purchase of the 20-year-old Patrick Vieira from AC Milan in 1996 signaled the beginning of the Arsène Wenger era at Arsenal.

Although not officially confirmed as manager, Wenger instructed the club to buy the central midfielder as he was on the verge of signing for Ajax. It proved one of the finest pieces of business the club has ever done. He made an immediate impression, coming on as a sub against Sheffield Wednesday to boss the midfield and turn the match around. He became a fixture in the team and the following season his partnership with fellow Frenchman Emmanuel Petit provided a bedrock that enabled the club to win the Premiership and FA Cup double. The season was capped by the two men combining for Petit to score France's third and last goal in the World Cup final against Brazil.

Vieira combined an athleticism that allowed him to get from box to box at pace with an uncanny ability to retain possession in the tightest of situations, frequently drawing free-kicks from frustrated opponents. Both a ballwinner and a distributor, he was a vital cog and the team never looked quite as effective in his absence. He became vice-captain to Tony Adams and due to injuries the skipper suffered in his final season – when the club recorded a second 'double' under Wenger – Vieira ended up leading the team more frequently than Adams.

> **ff Patrick was one of the greatest players in the club's history. His impact, not only at Arsenal but in English football overall, was tremendous**
> Arsène Wenger **JJ**

He was given the armband in his own right when Adams retired and there followed three consecutive trophy-winning seasons under the inspirational number 4, including the 'Invincibles' Premiership crown of 2003/04. Lee Dixon said of his influence on the squad, "They look up to him for his performances, but he is also the man to link the foreign players with the French and English players. He holds it all together." His last kick for the Gunners was the winner in the penalty shoot-out to decide the 2005 FA Cup final against Manchester United. With his departure the trophies dried up as Arsenal failed to successfully replace the man from Senegal.

Born: Dakar, Senegal, 23rd June 1976

Arsenal appearances: 406

Arsenal goals: 34

Honours won with Arsenal: Premiership (1998, 2002, 2004), FA Cup (1998, 2002, 2003, 2005)

Other clubs: Cannes (1993), AC Milan (1995), Juventus (2005), Inter Milan (2006)

International appearances: France, 107 caps, 6 goals

PATRICK VIEIRA FACTFILE

IAN WRIGHT

Ian Wright was brought to Arsenal early in September 1991 and scored a hat-trick on his league debut versus Southampton, before claiming the Golden Boot award that season with 29 league goals (five scored with Crystal Palace, for whom he started the campaign).

The 29th goal, that completed a hat-trick (ironically against Southampton), was the final one scored in front of the standing North Bank.

His prolific ability to find the net (he was the club's leading scorer for six consecutive campaigns) signaled a change in Arsenal's playing style as more creative players were sacrificed by boss George Graham in order for the team to play to Wright's strengths – his pace and lethal finishing. By concentrating on defence, the team became very difficult to score against and matches were often won thanks to Wright's goals. In his second season, he helped the club to win a domestic cup 'double'.

A year later, he cruelly missed the 1994 European Cup Winners' Cup final triumph, due to suspension. His sheer enthusiasm led to a yellow card in the semi-final second leg. He explained, "When I get into trouble on the pitch I'm so psyched up, wound up and pumped up because I want to do well, it overflows." Wright's personality was both loud and infectious and fans warmed to his demonstrative character. He wore his heart on his sleeve, a typical comment that sums up both a striker's mentality and the man's personality being when he admitted, "I'm desperate for goals: they're what my job is all about, and if I'm not scoring – even if the team is winning – I sulk."

He played for two seasons under Arsène Wenger, scoring his 179th Arsenal goal during the second to break the club's goalscoring record held by Cliff Bastin. However, he became injured in January 1998 and although his contribution to the League title that was secured four months on is undeniable, his absence demonstrated that the team could flourish without him and, at the age of 34, the manager decided Wright was dispensable.

> ❝ He's an instinctive player. His movements are perfect, so intelligent even when he has not got the ball. And that is why he scores the goals ❞
>
> Arsène Wenger

IAN WRIGHT FACTFILE

Born: Woolwich, London, 3 November 1963
Arsenal appearances: 288
Arsenal goals: 185
Honours won with Arsenal:
Premiership (1998), FA Cup (1993), League Cup (1993)
Other clubs: Crystal Palace (1985), West Ham (1998), Celtic (1999), Burnley (2000)
International appearances:
England, 33 caps, 9 goals

CHAPMAN THE INNOVATOR

Herbert Chapman was one of the greatest innovators in the game's history, and in less than a decade at Arsenal came up with several ideas which verify him as a football thinker years ahead of his time.

One of his most famous developments came very soon after his arrival at Highbury, when the team changed from the 2-3-5 formation to 3-4-3. A change in the offside law reducing the number of opposition players needed between the attacker and the goal line from three to two led Chapman to introduce a centre back to counter the opposing centre forward. The WM, as the formation came to be known, also allowed a greater balance between offensive and defensive play.

Other ideas soon followed. In August 1928, Arsenal were the first team to wear numbers on the back of their shirts. Chapman reasoned that if players were able to identify each other more quickly, it would speed moves up. However, it did not curry favour at the Football League, and after sporting numbers for a solitary match, the club was banned from repeating the experiment.

Chapman regarded the approach of those that

Chapman shaped not only Arsenal, but the game itself

ran the game as a huge cause of frustration. He wrote, "I appeal to the authorities to release the brake which they seem to delight in jamming on new ideas… as if wisdom is only to be found in the council chamber… I am impatient and intolerant of much that seems to me to be merely negative, if not actually destructive, legislation."

He advocated goal judges to decide on the issue of whether a ball actually crossed the goal line, a debate that continues to this day. He asserted, "We owe it to the public that our games should be controlled with all the exactness that is possible." He also advocated use of a white ball so that spectators could make it out more clearly.

Chapman, far right, shoots a round of golf with some of his Gunners in 1929

With Alex James, right, on the pitch at Wembley before the 1932 FA Cup final

Floodlit football was another innovation that was only adopted years later. Chapman had lights built into the West Stand to facilitate evening matches, but the Football Association insisted they could not be used for official matches. And thanks to Chapman, years before European competition, Arsenal were the first English team to regularly travel abroad to take part in showpiece friendlies, notably against Paris's Racing Club de France, who were first played in 1930.

Looking back, the suggestions seem eminently sensible, but Chapman's ideas were regarded as eccentric and off the wall in his own lifetime.

His team-talks were also revolutionary, as he encouraged players to contribute by expressing their own views. It was from this approach that the WM formation was developed. Chapman used a magnetic table on which a football pitch was marked out with tiny players that could be moved around. With the two-way discussion, all aspects of the forthcoming game were fully explored and every player was certain what would be required of them and what they might expect. The *Daily Mail* wrote of Chapman's approach, "Breaking down old traditions, he was the first club manager who set out methodically to organise the winning of matches."

More specific to his own club, Chapman introduced the now famous white sleeves to Arsenal's kit in 1934. Also, he introduced the idea of a giant clock for spectators to monitor how much of a match had been played and remained, leading to the labelling of Highbury's South Stand as the Clock End.

One proposal that was to go down in north London football folklore was to change the name of the underground station next to the club's Highbury Stadium from Gillespie Road to Arsenal. It was no small feat to persuade London Transport to effect the change, with all the signage that would need to be altered. Even today, after the stadium move, more people use Arsenal underground station to travel to home matches than any other. The legacies of football's great ideas man linger on over 70 years after his death.

Sir Jacob Epstein's bronze bust resided in Highbury for years, and it now adorns the Emirates' reception

THE STORY OF THE GUNNERS
GREATNESS BECKONS
1966-95

When Bertie Mee took over as manager in 1966, he inherited a squad of mainly young home-grown players who would bring success back to the club for the first time since the days of post-war austerity.

Although not regarded as a footballing mastermind, Mee's astute choice of first team coaches, Dave Sexton and later Don Howe, ignited the team. Under Mee, Arsenal once again reached Wembley, making it to the League Cup final two years running. In 1968 they lost to Leeds United, but were hot favourites against third division Swindon Town a year later. The Wembley pitch, however, had been reduced to a quagmire by the Horse of the Year show the previous week, and this combined with a flu epidemic at Highbury meant Arsenal failed to match their opponent's stamina on a heavy pitch, especially during extra time where Swindon ran out worthy 3-1 winners.

However, what followed proved the character of Mee's players. They reached the two-legged final of the Inter Cities Fairs Cup (soon to be re-branded the UEFA Cup) in 1970 against Belgium's Anderlecht. They were 3-0 down in the first leg in Brussels but a late consolation goal gave the team some hope. In the return leg at Highbury Arsenal needed a two-nil victory to win on away goals but an emphatic 3-0 triumph, reckoned by many to be the greatest night the old stadium ever witnessed, saw them home in style. A 17-year wait for a trophy was finally at an end.

More success came in 1970/71 as the club landed the double of League championship and FA Cup. The campaign culminated with the Gunners taking the First Division title courtesy of a 1–0 win at the home of neighbours Tottenham, thanks to a late Ray Kennedy header. Five days later the FA Cup final against Liverpool saw Wembley prove a happy hunting ground, even if it needed extra time to win

Physio Bertie Mee puts the players through their paces in a 1962 session at Highbury

Celebrations after the thrilling FA Cup final victory over Manchester United in 1979

the game. The attempt to defend the cup ended in a losing final appearance against Leeds in 1972, before Mee began to break up the double team, many felt too early. When the team narrowly avoided relegation in 1976, it was followed by Mee's resignation after a decade in the job.

The next manager, former captain Terry Neill, had been doing the job at Tottenham for two seasons. By this time the club's youth policy had produced a trio of good Irish players – Liam Brady, Frank Stapleton and David O'Leary. Neill brought both Pat Jennings and Willie Young with him from Tottenham and the team were soon reaching cup finals again – four between 1978 and 1980. Three were consecutive FA Cup final appearances, although the only victorious one was in 1979 against Manchester United. The 1979/80 season was especially cruel. Due to replays, the team played 70 matches that season. Four days after failing to retain the FA Cup against West Ham, they travelled to Brussels for the European Cup Winners' Cup final. A tight game against Valencia ended goalless but was lost in a penalty shoot-out.

The fans would have to wait seven years before
another final appearance, as Neill allowed key players
to leave, including Brady and Stapleton.

Neill was sacked in 1983 and coach Don Howe
promoted. He failed to improve the team's fortunes

and resigned in 1986 when he got wind that the club were trying to recruit Barcelona boss Terry Venables to replace him. That summer, it was former player George Graham that arrived instead.

Having impressed at Second Division Millwall, he gradually cleared most of the experienced stars from the club's books to ensure his authority was not

challenged by dissenting voices, with only David O'Leary remaining at the club from among the older heads. It paid dividends as Graham inherited a good crop of talent developed at the club, augmented by bargain signings from the lower divisions and less glamorous First Division opponents.

Silverware arrived in his first season via the League

Michael Thomas scores the famous last-gasp goal that secured the title at Anfield in 1989

Ian Wright celebrates in typical style after scoring in the 1993 FA Cup final

Cup, when firm favourites Liverpool were beaten by their much less experienced rivals. It was to provide a springboard for an even more significant game two years later, when the final fixture of the season saw Arsenal visit Liverpool needing to win by a two-goal margin to pip their hosts to the title. As the home team had dominated football for 15 years, few gave Graham's young team much chance. However, they bucked the odds to become champions in dramatic fashion, scoring the decisive second goal in the 90th minute.

Two years on another championship followed,

when Arsenal lost only one of their 38 matches. It was to be the team's final serious assault on the title under Graham, as they lacked consistency and changed their style to rely more on defence than creativity. Flair players were dropped, then sold, with the manager favouring a long ball game to create chances for new signing Ian Wright. The Gunners became more adept at cup football, if only because they were very difficult to beat in tight one-off matches.

A League Cup and FA Cup double was achieved in 1993, in both instances against Sheffield Wednesday, the FA Cup final involving a replay and extra time before a late winner for the Gunners as a penalty shoot-out beckoned.

A year later, Arsenal triumphed 1-0 in the European Cup Winners' Cup final, despite being underdogs against the holders, Italian side Parma. It was a dogged defensive display that epitomised what Arsenal had become.

Despite the cup successes, the team was in decline. The following season, when evidence came to light that Graham had been receiving some of the transfer fees that the club had paid to buy players, via a Norwegian agent, he was sacked. It was an echo of what had occurred in the 1920s with chairman Sir Henry Norris. Assistant Stewart Houston took over as caretaker boss and guided the team to another Cup Winners' Cup final, but this time, Arsenal were the victims of a late winner, scored by Spanish side Real Zaragoza.

ARSENAL COMIC STRIP HISTORY 3

IN THE LAST SEASON BEFORE WORLD WAR ONE, BOTH CHELSEA AND SPURS FINISHED IN THE RELEGATION POSITIONS IN DIVISION ONE...

BOTTOM...

	P	W	D	L	F	A	Pts.
	38	11	8			62	30
	38	9	12	17	46	65	29
Manchester U.	38	8	13	17	51	90	28
Chelsea	38	8	12	18	57		
Tottenham H.							

TOP OF... DIVISION 2

	P	W	D	L	F	A	Pts.
	38	23	7	8	71	33	53
Derby Co.	38	20	10	8	61	42	50
Preston N.E.	38	22	3	13	51	51	47
Barnsley	38	19	7	12	77	52	45
Wolverhampton W.	38	19	5	14	62	39	43
Birmingham	38	17	9		69	41	43
Arsenal	38	19	5	14	65	54	43

WHEN FOOTBALL RESUMED AFTER THE WAR, IT WAS DECIDED TO EXPAND THE FIRST DIVISION FROM 20 TEAMS TO 22...

SO... CHELSEA WILL NOT BE RELEGATED.

BUT SPURS?

ARSENAL'S SIR HENRY NORRIS 'PERSUADED' HIS FELLOW CHAIRMEN...

...THAT ARSENAL AND *NOT* SPURS SHOULD BE GIVEN A PLACE IN THE TOP FLIGHT. SPURS CLAIMED THAT *BRIBERY* WAS THE ONLY EXPLANATION FOR THEIR NEIGHBOURS' PROMOTION TO THE TOP DIVISION, WHERE THEY HAVE REMAINED EVER SINCE...

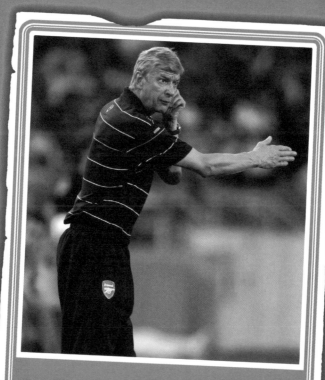

TACTICS

HERBERT CHAPMAN'S WM

In 1925, a change to the offside rule meant that only two opposing players (it had been three) were required to be between the most forward attacker and the goal to avoid being offside. As a consequence, many more goals were scored. In a team meeting after a 7-0 defeat, forward Charlie Buchan suggested, "Why not have a defensive centre half, or third full back, to block the gap down the middle?" Herbert Chapman shaped the future of football by adopting the idea and changing the traditional way teams of the time lined up.

So whereas 2-3-5 utilised two defenders and five forwards, the new 3-4-3 formation, which became known as the WM formation because of the shape of the team, offered an extra player in between the two full backs, making it more difficult for opposing forwards to score. Effectively, the centre half was moved back from midfield to become a centre back. Additionally, Chapman moved his two inside forwards deeper to provide a link between the five defensive-minded outfield players and those in attack.

As that would have left the centre forward isolated, the two wingers each moved a few yards inside, no longer hugging the touchline and looking to cut in when they received the ball (often from an inside forward during a lightning counter attack) rather than head for the goal-line to get in a cross.

The benefits for Arsenal came gradually, as Chapman honed the system and improved the quality of the players used via the transfer market. However, the glut of honours that the 1930s produced proved that 3-4-3 was the way forward and it was soon embraced by other clubs.

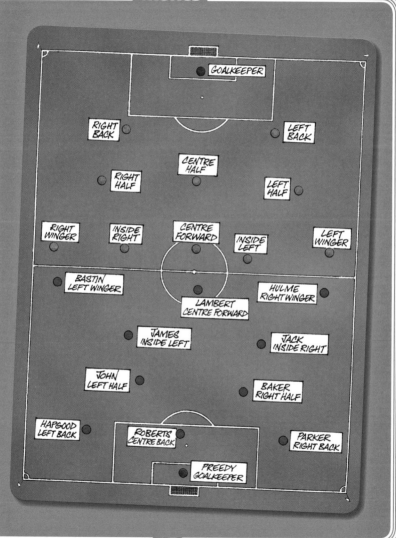

THE CLASSIC OFFSIDE TRAP

One tactic that has, at different times, been synonymous with Arsenal has been the use of the offside trap. Although Arsenal could not be credited with devising the tactic itself, it was Herbert Chapman's use of a third centre back played slightly behind the full backs which gave the team the opportunity to deploy a very effective line.

Future Gunners teams continued to use the tactic, as did every other side once its advantages became obvious. However, it was probably at its most potent when George Graham put together the back four of Nigel Winterburn, Tony Adams, Steve Bould and Lee Dixon in the late 1980s. Their understanding was such that they were rarely caught out and often compressed play by keeping a high line. This, especially at free kicks, helped ease the pressure on the keeper.

David Seaman said of the 1994 Cup Winners' Cup final, "That was the one time I really enjoyed the offside rule. We were just holding the box and every time they were running in they got caught offside." The trap played its part in the 1990/91 championship, when only 18 goals were conceded in 38 league games.

The tactic was successful so often that, in the eyes of many opposition fans, the eternal image of Tony Adams is with his arm raised appealing to the linesman for a decision. "There have been a lot of jokes about that," says Lee Dixon, "like the Arsenal Subbuteo team with the back four having their hands in the air."

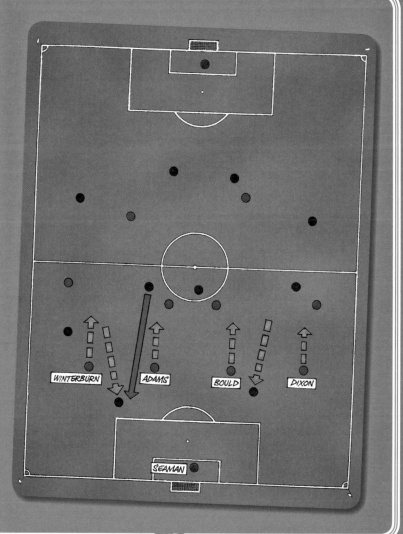

WINTERBURN

ADAMS

BOULD

DIXON

SEAMAN

GRAHAM'S DEFENSIVE MASTERCLASS

When Arsenal reached the 1994 European Cup Winners' Cup final against holders Parma in Copenhagen, the Italian side were clear favourites to retain the trophy, not least because the Gunners had their key men Ian Wright and John Jensen unavailable. But the team had become adept at winning big one-off matches through determined defending, and ultimately George Graham's tactics proved the difference between the sides.

He was able to field his trusted backline of Lee Dixon, Steve Bould, Tony Adams and Nigel Winterburn in front of David Seaman, with a five-man midfield in front of them. The wide players were instructed to funnel attacks into the centre, where the crowded midfield and two combative centre backs meant that, in the words of Alan Smith, Parma, "weren't allowed to play at all".

Parma may have had superior technical players in Gianfranco Zola, Faustino Asprilla and Tomas Brolin but, denied room, could not make it count. Tony Adams remembers, "We won by tangling them up in a spider's web."

It was the season that the '1-0 to the Arsenal' chant was born, and there was no better demonstration of it than this game. The Gunners only needed to score once and then rely on their men at the back. Smith scored the required goal in the 20th minute. He reflects today, "It was the pinnacle of that back four's effectiveness. Once I'd scored, it was all about them. They were just awesome that night."

The remainder of the final was a defensive masterclass. As George Graham recalled, "Once we went a goal in front I knew we had a chance because our strength was keeping clean sheets."

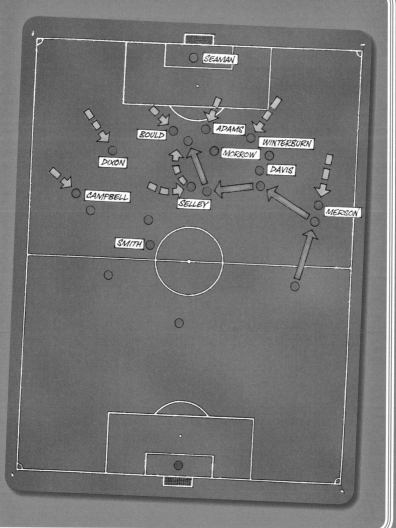

WENGER'S LIGHTNING FAST TOTAL FOOTBALL

Arsene Wenger's football philosophy is to play "a game based on technical skill, mobility, dynamism and creativity" He attempts to build teams that feature players embodying all of these traits, and when he has achieved this, Arsenal win silverware.

He recruits players he believes can express his idea of 'total football' – a concept whose origins lie in the Ajax team of the early 1970s – but Wenger adds the twist of supreme pace. The Ajax-developed Dennis Bergkamp described Arsenal's football in the team that won five major trophies between 2002 and 2005 as "the closest I have seen to the Dutch concept of total football".

Wenger's favoured qualities were encapsulated by a goal in the match at White Hart Lane that sealed the Premiership in 2004. Forward Thierry Henry carried the ball out of defence after a Tottenham corner into the opposition half. There, he read the run of Bergkamp, hugging the left wing, to the corner of the penalty area. The Dutchman took just one touch to send the ball into the path of onrushing midfielder Patrick Vieira, who had run the length of the pitch, to connect and score.

It mattered not which position the players were supposed to fill, all had licence to play with expression as and where they saw fit, and at breakneck speed if required, all the while with an almost telepathic understanding of the space their team-mates would run into. At times, they were simply unplayable. Leeds's Olivier Dacourt described playing Wenger's team as "demoralising. They just pass and move, pass and move. You find yourself working for nothing."

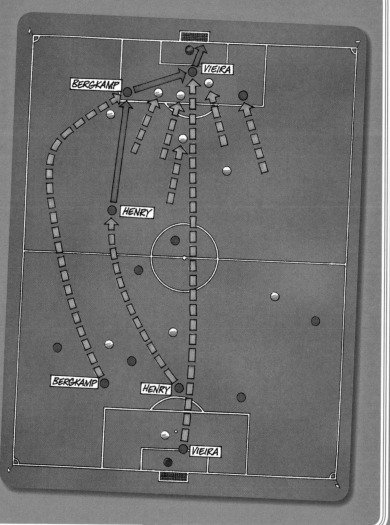

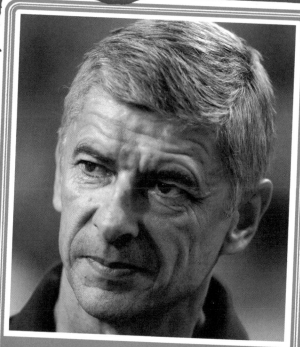

GREAT
GAFFERS

Herbert Chapman was the first manager to win a major trophy for Arsenal, the 1930 FA Cup, and he transformed the club into one of the greatest names of English football history.

A visionary in all aspects of the game, Chapman ensured the fitness of his team was superior to others, at the same time as treating them with more respect than was normally afforded to footballers. In this way he did what he could to get the best from his players physically, mentally, technically and tactically.

George Allison consulted the players closely...

Arriving from reigning champions Huddersfield in 1925, he constantly looked to strengthen his side, and despite taking the club to its first FA Cup final in 1927 it was not until Chapman was given significant funds to bring in better players that Arsenal became a major force. The seven trophies won in the 1930s suggest the club could have won even more if they'd speculated to accumulate more in his early seasons at Highbury. Chapman passed away in January 1934 due to pneumonia after watching three matches in three days, having refused to rest on developing a cold. Proof indeed of his dedication to the club and his job.

George Allison was the club's managing director and took over as manager. Chapman's assistant and future club secretary Bob Wall said that Allison, "never claimed to possess a deep theoretical knowledge of the game but he listened closely to what people like Tom Whittaker and Alex James had to say. He always insisted that he would secure a prospective signing only if his character was beyond reproach."

His purchase of key players such as Ted Drake and Wilf Copping continued his predecessor's aim of constantly improving the team and Arsenal's success did not

...a productive approach continued by his successor Tom Whittaker

Bertie Mee's
disciplinarian approach
took his team to
Double success

abate until the outbreak of World War Two. But by
the time football recommenced, the team needed
rebuilding and Allison only managed for one more
season before retiring.

He handed the reins over to physio (and former
player) Tom Whittaker and the results were immediate.
Arsenal regained the League Championship during his
first season in charge and there followed an FA Cup
and a further title in the next five years. Whittaker had a
polite but effective manner with the players. Joe Mercer
described him as "the greatest man I ever met".
However, he was unable to match the sustained success
of the 1930s as he found it difficult to attract major
stars. He died of a heart attack in 1956 and the club
then employed a succession of managers, all of whom
failed to bring success.

That changed with the promotion of another Arsenal physio to the manager's post. Bertie Mee took over in 1966 and developed a young group of players that would eventually bring success back to the club. Mee had a military air about him and allowed no slacking, with a frequently stated purpose of "stopping mediocrity being perpetuated". He employed great coaches in Dave Sexton and Don Howe and bought necessary players astutely to build a side that peaked with the 1971 League and FA Cup 'double', something even the great team of the 1930s had failed to achieve.

Mee knew how to get the best from his players, building his side on the basis of youthful camaraderie and intense effective teamwork rather than reliance on prima donnas. However, there was criticism that his double-winning side were boring, which perhaps played a part in his allowing some squad members to leave when they could have served the club better than those who replaced them. Mee resigned in 1976 as Arsenal failed to build on their 1971 success, and the departure of Howe after the double season may well have been a key factor in this respect. Mee's replacement

Terry Neill achieved Cup success but fell out with some of his squad

The players called George Graham 'Gaddafi' and his approach dictated success

Terry Neill, in spite of building a team of talented players, only managed to land a solitary FA Cup in seven seasons.

Former player George Graham arrived from managing Millwall in 1986 and, echoing the ways of Mee, whom he had served under, rebuilt the team with a mix of the youngsters on the club's books and bargain buys, some from lower divisions. His disciplinarian ways were in huge contrast to his playing days. David O'Leary later claimed that "George liked his Gaddafi reputation", a reference to the nickname the players gave him due to his dictatorial approach. If he ruled by fear, the early results were impressive, with two titles and a League Cup under his belt in his first five seasons.

However, concentration on replicating the ethos of the 1971 double team – "If you weren't working hard, you weren't playing," remembers Paul Merson – resulted in creative players becoming something of a luxury, and the team's ability to win matches consistently declined. The players were still able to grind out results selectively, and in the latter stages of

Graham's time three cups were won. However the 'bung' scandal in the autumn of 1994 signalled the end of his era a few months later.

Arsène Wenger's arrival in 1996 proved a breath of fresh air, as he set about transforming the reputation of Arsenal and ultimately its physical surroundings – namely state of the art training facilities and the move to a new stadium in 2006. His impact on both the club and English football proved as significant as Chapman's decades earlier, with a new, more scientific approach to the fitness and conditioning of footballers, as well as the utilisation of a far greater number of foreign imports than before his arrival.

Arsène Wenger totally transformed the club, elevating it to its greatest heights

Arsenal benefited through both trophies – seven between 1998 and 2005 – and a fabulous footballing style that resulted in invariable sell-outs, even in the new 60,000-seater stadium. As Champions League football has become financially imperative, Wenger has ensured continuous qualification for the tournament for over a decade, no mean feat considering the financial restrictions under which he has had to operate. He has secured the club's status as one of the world's elite group of superclubs, and testimony to his reputation is the constant courting by Real Madrid.

MEMORABLE
MATCHES

ARSENAL 3 ANDERLECHT 0

Inter-Cities Fairs Cup final 1970, 2nd Leg, Highbury, London, 28th April 1970

Having lost finals in the each of the previous two seasons, Arsenal were hoping it was a case of third time lucky when they qualified for the European Fairs Cup final in 1970, taking the notable scalp of the Johan Cruyff-inspired Ajax en route, alongside those of Glentoran, Sporting Lisbon, Rouen and Dinamo Bacau.

Finals in this competition were two-legged affairs at the time, and the first match against their opponents, Belgian team Anderlecht, took place in Brussels.

Arsenal were over-run by the home side – "They murdered us, if they had scored six we couldn't have complained" said winger George Armstrong – and found themselves 3-0 down after 74 minutes. An 18-year-old Ray Kennedy came on as a substitute, and scored what many felt was a consolation goal, although it later proved far more significant.

The second leg took place at Highbury two weeks later, with

Arsenal requiring a 2-0 victory to win the tie on the away goals rule. The atmosphere in the stadium that night has gone down in Arsenal legend, as a vociferous crowd willed on the team. Having been starved of a trophy since 1953, the fans needed little motivation to give their all to encourage the players. George Armstrong described it as "the best atmosphere I've ever seen, a full house and about 40,000 outside that couldn't get in. The terraces were packed, like our 12th man." It appeared to have an effect, as Arsenal kept a clean sheet while scoring three times through Eddie Kelly, John Radford and Jon Sammels.

Anderlecht had 14 minutes to bring the scores level and force extra time, but Arsenal held firm to end the club's longest spell without a major trophy since they won their first under Herbert Chapman in 1930.

A mass pitch invasion after the presentation of the trophy saw Frank McLintock being chaired around the pitch by happy supporters. The same group of players would go on to win the league and cup double the following season, and the Fairs Cup was a vital stepping stone to that achievement.

John Radford (far post) celebrates the vital second goal on a barnstorming night at Highbury

Arsenal:
Wilson, Storey, McLintock, Simpson, McNab, Armstrong, Kelly, Sammels, Graham, Radford, George,

Scorers:
Kelly, Radford, Sammels

Attendance:
51, 612

LIVERPOOL 0 ARSENAL 2

Football League First Division, Anfield, Liverpool, 26th May 1989

After leading the 1988/89 First Division Championship for much of the season, Arsenal wobbled as they came into the final straight.

Arsenal celebrate snatching the title in an extraordinary final game at Anfield

The game against the Liverpool team chasing them had been scheduled for Sunday 23rd April, too early to be decisive. However, the Hillsborough tragedy in which many Liverpool fans lost their lives meant the fixture was rescheduled for the last Friday in May.

By this time, Liverpool's superior form meant the Gunners found themselves in second place, needing to win at Anfield by a two-goal margin to take the title they looked to have thrown away. Manager George Graham began the match by fielding a 5-3-2 formation, mindful of how important it was that his team did not concede a goal. Not needing to win, "Liverpool played into our hands," Graham remembers,

the home side content to play the game out rather than perform to their capabilities. At half time it was scoreless, although the Arsenal boss was perfectly happy as he had predicted the necessary goals would come after the interval.

He was proved correct, as the visitors took the lead thanks to an indirect free kick after 55 minutes. Nigel Winterburn floated the ball in and striker Alan Smith made contact with the side of his head to divert the ball into the net. The Liverpool players furiously appealed the goal was illegal, but to no avail.

As injury time neared, the chances of the vital second goal looked slim, but a long ball pumped forward to Alan Smith was knocked on to midfielder Mickey Thomas, who received a lucky deflection off opposing defender Steve Nicol before regaining control and honing in on the goal. ITV commentator Brian Moore famously said, "It's up for grabs now!" as Thomas shaped to shoot, chipping the ball over diving keeper Bruce Grobbelaar just before the Liverpool defenders could catch him.

"I just waited for Bruce to make the first move, like a game of chess," recalls Thomas, "and then it was down to me." Arsenal had won the championship in the most dramatic finale the competition had ever witnessed.

Arsenal: Lukic, Dixon, Bould, (Groves), O'Leary, Adams, Winterburn, Rocastle, Thomas, Richardson, Merson (Hayes), Smith,

Scorers:
Smith, Thomas

Attendance:
41,783

MANCHESTER UNITED 0
ARSENAL 1

Premiership, Old Trafford, Manchester,
14th March 1998

The 1997/98 season was Arsène Wenger's first as Arsenal manager, and in the summer before the campaign he began to shake up his squad, letting English players such as Paul Merson go while signing foreign talents including Marc Overmars and Emmanel Petit.

Initially, there seemed little improvement, with the team 13 points behind leaders Manchester United by December.

However, in the league and FA Cup, the team found their form after the New Year and put together a run of 26 unbeaten games. The match that proved decisive in their assault on the title was the visit to Old Trafford in March. At the end of the previous season, United manager Alex Ferguson had said of the Arsenal boss, "He's a novice - he should keep his opinions to Japanese football." The wait for his words to come back and haunt him did not last long.

Needing to make up ground to have any chance of overtaking United, it was a must win game for the visitors, who took the game to

their opponents accordingly. Marc Overmars caused havoc on the right side of United's defence up against rookie John Curtis, who was subbed after seven minutes of the second half. As Overmars was denied a cast iron penalty and went close three times, it seemed the Gunners were destined not to claim the necessary three points.

The entrance of French teenage substitute Nicolas Anelka helped to break the deadlock. In the 78th minute, a ball played up to Dennis Bergkamp was flicked on to Anelka, whose header put Overmars clear of the defence. His pace ensured he would not be caught and this time he beat keeper Peter Schmeichel from the angle. "He showed he's a big game player," Wenger said of Overmars afterwards.

The victory gave Arsenal the belief they could win the club's first title since 1991. "Why shouldn't we win the title? If we win our games in hand, we are ahead," said Overmars. The team duly won their next eight matches, making up a further six points on United, to secure the Premiership trophy with two fixtures to spare.

Arsenal:
Manninger, Dixon, Keown, Adams, Winterburn, Parlour (Garde), Vieira, Petit, Overmars, Bergkamp, Wreh (Anelka)

Scorers:
Overmars

Attendance:
55,174

REAL MADRID 0 ARSENAL 1

Champions League Round of 16, First Leg, Estadio Santiago Bernabéu, Madrid, 21st February 2006

Under Arsène Wenger, Arsenal had enjoyed eight consecutive seasons of Champions League football, but by the quirk of the draw had never faced one particular continental giant until the 2005/06 competition. Then, in the first knockout round, they were paired with the legendary Real Madrid.

It was a tie Gooners had waited years for, the away game akin to a pilgrimage and tickets were like gold dust. Arsenal's defence had been ravaged by injuries, with three of the first choice players absent, yet the team surprised the travelling fans as they more than matched a Real side including such luminaries as Zinedine Zidane, Ronaldo, David Beckham, Raul and Roberto Carlos. In contrast to their hosts, the Gunners blended experience and youth in their line-up but there was no indication of stage fright. Wenger's team, with five in midfield, hustled

their hosts out of their stride, surprising the locals who had expected to see the customary attacking football from the men in white. In fact it was Arsenal who did the majority of the foraying forward, as their midfield supported the lone striker consistently. "You see that as soon as Arsenal is not scared to play, we can play good football," said captain Thierry Henry afterwards.

Thierry Henry capped a wonderful display with a fine goal

In one of his best ever performances for the club, it was he who settled the evening with a wonder goal in the 47th minute. Collecting the ball from Cesc Fabregas close to the centre circle, his pace took him past four defenders before he scored with a low shot across keeper Iker Casillas. It was one of many attempts, and Wenger's words afterwards – "My only regret is that we did not add one or two more goals" – indicated just how good Arsenal had been as they became the first English side to win at the Bernabéu.

A dramatic return leg ended goalless, and Real were eliminated, in spite of their stellar line-up. Henry's strike in Madrid proved the key moment, a huge step in a campaign that would end with Arsenal's first ever Champions League final appearance, ironically in the striker's home city of Paris.

Arsenal:
Lehmann, Eboue, Toure, Senderos, Flamini, Ljungberg, Fabregas (Song), Gilberto, Hleb (Pires), Reyes (Diaby), Henry

Scorers: Henry

Attendance: 80,000

ARSENAL COMIC STRIP HISTORY 4

SEPTEMBER 2002...ARSENE WENGER, MANAGER OF THE DEFENDING CHAMPIONS, IS GIVING A PRESS CONFERENCE...

IT WILL BE DIFFICULT FOR US TO GO THROUGH THE SEASON UNBEATEN, BUT WE CAN DO IT.

A MONTH LATER THE GUNNERS LOSE A PREMIERSHIP MATCH FOR THE FIRST TIME SINCE DECEMBER 2001...

SPURS WIN: ARSENAL LOSE AT EVE AS

COMICAL WENGER SAYS WE CAN GO THROUGH THE WHOLE SEASON UNBEATEN...

SOON A T-SHIRT IS PRODUCED LAMPOONING WENGER IN THE STYLE OF THE IRAQI INFORMATION MINISTER KNOWN AS 'COMICAL ALI'...

BUT WENGER HAS THE LAST LAUGH WHEN, A SEASON LATER, ARSENAL WIN THE TITLE UNDEFEATED...

...AND A FAN GIVES HIM ONE OF THE SHIRTS AS THE TEAM PARADE THE TROPHY AFTER THE FINAL HOME GAME!

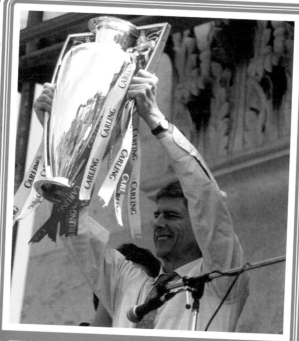

THE STORY OF THE GUNNERS
WENGER'S ARSENAL
1995-2009

In the 1995 close season, Arsenal unveiled the then Bolton boss Bruce Rioch as the man to succeed George Graham. He was the first Arsenal manager since Billy Wright in the 1960s without previous links to the club.

His first few weeks saw superstars Dennis Bergkamp and David Platt join from the Italian league. With such big names on board, it was expected that the team would do better than the fifth-place they achieved, but they didn't and Rioch departed. It later transpired that the next manager, Frenchman Arsène Wenger, might have been given the job earlier had some directors been less cautious about hiring a continental who lacked experience of the English game. That they had the opportunity to reverse that decision in 1996 was a major turning point in the club's history.

Having only managed in France and Japan, Arsène Wenger was almost completely unknown, with London's *Evening Standard* carrying the headline 'Arsène Who?' when news came through that he was Rioch's successor. Yet he transformed both the team and the English footballing culture whilst extending the careers of an experienced defence that had gone off the boil somewhat towards the end of George Graham's reign. He achieved this while also rebuilding both midfield and attack with imported bargains to make the club a dominant force in Premiership football.

Dennis Bergkamp, arguably the single most pivotal player in modern Arsenal history

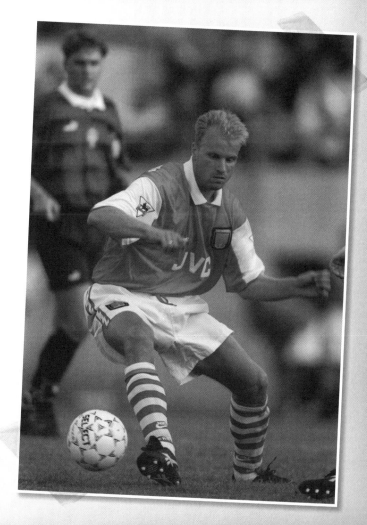

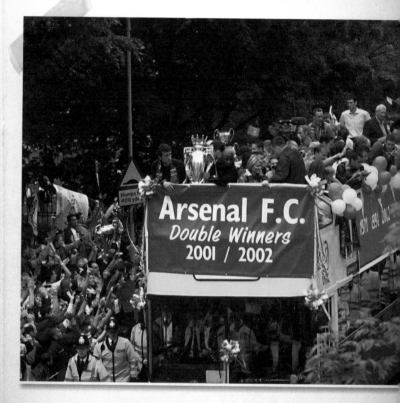

Arsenal's all-conquering men and women parade their trophy haul down Islington's Upper Street

Wenger guided the team to third place in his first season, despite arriving part way through due to his contractual commitments to Japan's Grampus Eight. In his first full campaign Arsenal won the League and FA Cup double. For the next seven seasons, the club would never finish outside the top two, an incredible

achievement given how little money the manager spent. Quite apart from having an eye for fine players that he could improve further, Wenger would often turn a significant profit when players left the club.

Among the stars from the era that proved to be bargain buys were Patrick Vieira, Marc Overmars, Emmanuel Petit, Nicolas Anelka, Thierry Henry and Robert Pires. All departed for teams in Spain or Italy and aside from Pires, who was out of contract, commanded huge fees, allowing Wenger to buy cheaper replacements.

After Wenger's first double, Arsenal remained competitive in both league and cups, but it was four years before the next trophy arrived. However, the fabulous football being played was invariably packing out the 38,500 capacity Highbury stadium, despite ever-increasing ticket prices. So the directors decided the club required a new stadium to allow more fans to see matches and increase turnover to pay for the best players. Their existing stadium could not be expanded sufficiently due to the surrounding housing, but a new site, Ashburton Grove – at the centre of which Islington's rubbish was processed – was found a few hundred metres west to allow the club to remain in the area. Having already proved a prudent operator in the transfer market, the manager would now have no choice, as the club took out huge loans to fund the building of their new home.

While the new stadium was under construction, Arsenal enjoyed a memorable four seasons in which they won the league twice (2002 and 2004) and the FA Cup three times (2002, 2003 and 2005 – all in Cardiff, as Wembley was being rebuilt). Wenger's players peaked for the 2003/04 title in which their crowning achievement was to remain unbeaten over the course of the entire league campaign. That team became known as 'The Invincibles' and with matches in the seasons before and after, put together a record total of 49 league games without defeat. It was a phenomenal achievement, not least because they continued to play attacking football that was pleasing on the eye.

In 2005/06 came the club's final season at Highbury, and fans also saw the team progress to a Champions League final against Barcelona. They were unfortunate to be reduced to ten men early in the game when their Spanish opponents scored, only for the referee to award a foul instead and dismiss Arsenal's keeper Jens Lehmann. Despite this, Arsenal took the lead, only to be worn down by their opponents and eventually lose 2-1. The competition that year had provided some memorable nights at Highbury, with matches against Real Madrid and Juventus giving the old stadium a fantastic send off. The last European fixture

Fans say goodbye to Highbury on 7 May 2006. That fella in the crowd looks familiar...

Supporters flock to see the team at the club's new home, the Emirates Stadium, in greater numbers than ever

staged was a semi-final first leg against Villarreal, remembered for the famous 'Highbury squirrel' running around the pitch for several minutes as play continued.

The Highbury story had a happy ending with the very final match seeing Arsenal pip neighbours Tottenham to fourth place in the league, and the attendant financially crucial Champions League qualification. Tottenham only had to win at West Ham, but their team came down with food poisoning and were unable to achieve the required victory. It enabled Gunners' fans to see their team win the final game at the historic stadium (against Wigan) whilst celebrating the misfortunes of their local rivals on a glorious May day.

Wenger gradually let most of the Invincibles team depart over the course of three seasons as he rebuilt his side while the club moved the short distance to their new home, the 60,000 capacity Emirates Stadium. Financial restrictions began to bite as the manager had to prove even more spendthrift, meaning a policy of buying younger, less proven players and allowing them to develop in the first team.

Despite this, they still offered hope that they could compete with their freer-spending rivals, coming close to winning the title in 2008 and reaching the Champions League semi-finals in 2009 before falling short. And the new stadium, despite the increased capacity, is almost always sold out. The challenge for Arsene Wenger and the manager that follows is to continue giving supporters a reason to buy the highly priced tickets, at the same time as the club continues to pay off the huge loan required to build the new home. After all, the reason for the move is to ensure the club's future is one of guaranteed prosperity, on and off the field.

THE BATTLE OF HIGHBURY

On 14th November 1934, a match took place at Highbury stadium that has gone down in Arsenal legend, despite being an international friendly fixture between England and recently crowned World Cup winners Italy. As England did not enter the tournament for the first time until 1950, it was labeled "the real World Cup final" in the English press, and was Italy's first match since winning the trophy in Paris. Italian Prime Minister Benito Mussolini reportedly offered each of the national team's players an Alfa Romeo car and a substantial bonus payment if they won.

Five of the seven Arsenal players who lined up for England (from left) Copping, Hapgood, Moss, Bowden, Bastin

However, what occurred could also fuel the argument that the Arsenal side of this period was the best team on the planet, as all but four of those selected to represent England were Gunners' players. They had

won two consecutive league titles and were in the process of securing a third. Seven players from one club starting an England international set a record that has not been eclipsed. They were Frank Moss, George Male, Eddie Hapgood, Wilf Copping, Ray Bowden, Ted Drake and Cliff Bastin. A young winger named Stanley Matthews won his third cap, and that none of those on duty had made ten international appearances was testimony to the inexperience of the line-up.

The game became known as The Battle of Highbury due to the violence of the encounter. Matthews later described it as the most violent game of his career, which lasted a further 30 years. It was indicative that the man of the match was hard man Copping, for his

Led by legendary manager Vittorio Pozzo (far left), the Italians line up before a training session at White Hart Lane

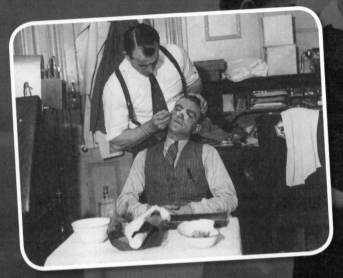

Arsenal trainer Tom Whittaker tends to Eddie Hapgood's broken nose after the bloody battle

battling display in midfield. England fittingly lined up in the 3-4-3 formation that Herbert Chapman had introduced at Arsenal, against Italy's more traditional 2-5-3. Eight of their players were drawn from two clubs – Inter and Juventus, so there was plenty of familiarity in their roster.

The nature of the contest was set from the start, with an early challenge from Ted Drake breaking the foot of opposition centre half Luis Monti. After two minutes, and decades before substitutes existed, Italy were down to ten men. They did not take kindly to losing their man to a bad tackle, and retaliated in kind. Among the injuries suffered by English players were a broken nose for Hapgood (who missed 15 minutes of the match while being treated), a damaged ankle for Bowden and a fractured arm for Manchester City striker Eric Brook. Drake was also punched. If Arsene Wenger frets about the danger of his players being injured on international duty, a history lesson might prove enlightening.

Despite the aggressive nature of the afternoon, England were focused enough to take advantage of their extra man, with two goals from Brook (after he had missed a penalty), followed up by another courtesy of Drake to give the home country a convincing lead. Italy rallied after the interval, Giuseppe Meazza scoring twice, hitting the woodwork and forcing some fine saves from Moss. England may have won 3-2, but due to their playing almost the entire match a man down, the losers were still feted back home, and are celebrated in Italian soccer folklore as The Lions of Highbury.

The game took place 20 years before the European Champions Cup was conceived. Real Madrid's reputation was built on their domination of the competition in its early days, as later those of Ajax, Real Madrid, Liverpool and AC Milan would be. The Battle of Highbury was persuasive evidence that, if it had existed in the 1930s, Arsenal would have enjoyed a similar period of domination over Europe as they had over England.

ENGLAND 3 ITALY 2

Friendly International, Highbury, London, 14th November 1934

England:
Moss, Male, Barker (Derby), Hapgood, Britton (Everton), Copping, Bowen, Bastin, Matthews (Stoke), Drake, Brook (Manchester City)

Scorers:
Brook 2, Drake

Attendance:
56,044

HONOURS AND RECORDS

MAJOR HONOURS

WINNERS

Football League Champions: 1931, 1933, 1934, 1935, 1938, 1948, 1953, 1971, 1989, 1991

Premier League Champions: 1998, 2002, 2004

FA Cup: 1930, 1936, 1950, 1971, 1979, 1993, 1998, 2002, 2003, 2005

League Cup: 1987, 1993

European Inter-Cities Fairs Cup: 1970

European Cup Winners' Cup: 1994

Charity/Community Shield: 1930, 1931, 1933, 1934, 1938, 1948, 1953, 1991 (shared), 1998, 1999, 2002, 2004

FA Youth Cup: 1966, 1971, 1988, 1994, 2000, 2001, 2009

RUNNERS-UP

Football League: 1926, 1932, 1973

Premier League: 1999, 2000, 2001, 2003, 2005

FA Cup: 1927, 1932, 1952, 1972, 1978, 1980, 2001

League Cup: 1968, 1969, 1988, 2007

UEFA Champions League: 2006

UEFA Cup: 2000

European Cup Winners' Cup: 1980, 1995

RECORDS

COMPETITION/INTERNATIONAL RECORDS

- Most consecutive seasons in English top flight: 84 (up to 2009/10)
- **Longest unbeaten sequence in English top flight: 49 matches (May 2003 - Oct 2004)**
- Longest unbeaten away sequence in English league football: 27 matches (5th April 2003 - 25th Sept 2004)
- **Most consecutive scoring league games in English domestic football: 55 (19th May 2001 - 30th Nov 2002)**
- Most consecutive scoring away games: 27 (19th May 2001 - 23rd Nov 2002)
- **Most players from one club in an England starting line-up: 7 (14th Nov 1934 v Italy)**
- Youngest player to play for England: Theo Walcott, 17 years 75 days (30th May 2006, England v Hungary)
- **Highest League attendance : 83,260 (Manchester United v Arsenal, at Maine Road, First Division, 17th Jan 1948)**
- Most consecutive league wins: 14 (Feb - Aug 2002)
- **Most consecutive away league matches unbeaten: 27 (5th April 2003 - 24th Oct 2004)**
- Fewest failures to score in a league season: 0 (Scored in every game), 2001/02
- **Most away league goals scored in a season: 60, 1930/31**
- Fastest goal by a substitute: 1.8 seconds, Nicklas Bendtner (v Tottenham Hotspur, 22nd Dec 2007)
- **Most consecutive matches in the Champions League without**

conceding a goal: 10 (18th Oct
2005-26 April 2006)

CLUB RECORDS

- Highest Home Attendance: (Highbury)
  73,295 v Sunderland, 9th Mar, 1935;
  (Wembley) 73,707 v Lens, 25th Nov
  1998; (Emirates) 60,161 v Manchester
  United, 3rd Nov, 2007
- **Biggest home win: 12-0 v
  Loughborough Town, 12th March
  1900 (Division 2) & v Ashford
  United, 14th Oct 1893 (FA Cup)**
- Biggest away win: 7-0 v Standard
  Liege, 3rd Nov 1993 (European Cup
  Winners' Cup)
- All competitions consecutive wins:
  14 (12th Sept 1987 - 21st Nov 1987)
- Consecutive Football League wins:
  10 (12th Sept 1987 - 21st Nov 1987)
- **Consecutive Premiership wins: 14
  (10th Feb 2002 - 24th Aug 2002)**
- Consecutive matches unbeaten: 28 (9th
  April 2007 - 24 Nov 2007)
- **Consecutive Football League
  matches unbeaten: 26 (28th April
  1990 - 2nd Feb 1991)**
- Consecutive Premiership matches
  unbeaten: 49 (7th May 2003 - 1st
  Feb 2005)
- **Consecutive Premiership matches
  scoring: 55 (19th May 2001 - 7th
  Dec 2002)**
- Most league wins in a season: 29 in
  42 matches, First Division, 1970/71
- **Most league goals scored in a
  season: 127 in 42 matches, First
  Division, 1930/31**

- Most points in a league season (2
  for a win): 66 in 42 matches, First
  Division, 1930/31
- **Most points in a league season (3
  for a win): 90 in 38 matches,
  Premier League, 2003/04**

INDIVIDUAL RECORDS
FOOTBALLER OF THE YEAR
1950: Joe Mercer
1971: Frank McLintock
1998: Dennis Bergkamp
2002: Robert Pires
2003, 2004, 2006: Thierry Henry

PLAYERS' PLAYER OF THE YEAR
1979: Liam Brady
1998: Dennis Bergkamp
2003, 2004: Thierry Henry

PLAYERS' YOUNG PLAYER
1987: Tony Adams
1989: Paul Merson
1999: Nicolas Anelka
2008: Cesc Fabregas

FOOTBALL LEAGUE DIVISION ONE/
PREMIER LEAGUE TOP SCORERS
1934/35: Ted Drake (42 goals)
1947/48: Ronnie Rooke (33)
1976/77: Malcolm Macdonald (25)
1988/89: Alan Smith (23)
1990/91: Alan Smith (23)
1991/92: Ian Wright (29)
2001/02: Thierry Henry (24)
2003/04: Thierry Henry (30)
2004/05: Thierry Henry (25)
2005/06: Thierry Henry (27)

CLUB INDIVIDUAL RECORDS

- Most overall appearances: 722, David O'Leary (1975 - 1993)
- **Most league appearances: 558, David O'Leary (1975 - 1993)**
- Most Premiership appearances: 333, Ray Parlour (1992 - 2004)
- **Most European appearances: 78, Thierry Henry (1999 - 2007)**
- Most Champions League appearances: 70, Thierry Henry (1999 - 2007)
- **Most consecutive appearances: 172, Tom Parker (Apr 1926 - Dec 1929)**
- Youngest Player: Cesc Fabregas (16 years 177 days, League Cup v Rotherham Utd, 28th Oct 2003)
- **Oldest Player: Jock Rutherford (41 years 159 days, v Man City, 20th March 1926)**
- Record Goalscorer: 214, Thierry Henry
- **Most League goals: 164, Thierry Henry**
- Most FA Cup goals: 26, Cliff Bastin
- **Most League Cup goals: 29, Ian Wright**
- Most European goals: 41, Thierry Henry
- **Most goals in a season (all competitions): 44, Ted Drake 1934/35 (42 League, 1 FA Cup, 1 Charity Shield)**
- Most goals in one match: 7, Ted Drake (v Aston Villa, away, 14th Dec 1935, won 7-1, League)
- **Fastest recorded goal: 20.07 seconds, Gilberto v PSV, away, 25 Sept 2002)**
- Youngest goalscorer: Cesc Fabregas, (16 years 212 days v Wolves, League Cup, 2nd Dec 2003)
- **Youngest hat-trick scorer: John Radford (17 years 315 days v Wolves, League, 2nd Jan 1965)**
- Oldest goalscorer: Jock Rutherford, 39 years 352 days v Sheffield United, League, 20th Sept 1924)
- **Most capped player while playing for the club: Thierry Henry, 81 caps for France**
- Most capped England player while playing for the club: Kenny Sansom, 77 caps

FIRSTS AND LASTS

- First match: v. Eastern Wanderers, Friendly, 11th Dec 1886 (won 6-0)
- **First match as Professionals: v Sheff United, 5th Sept 1891 (lost 0-2)**
- First League match: v Newcastle United, Second Division, 2nd Sept 1893 (drew 2-2)
- **First match in First Division: v Newcastle United, 3rd Sept 1904 (lost 3-0)**
- First overseas tour match: v Belgian XI in Brussels, 5th May 1906 (won 2-1)
- **First match at Highbury: v Leicester Fosse, Second Division, 16th Sept 1913 (won 2-1)**
- First European match: v Stævnet (Copenhagen XI), Fairs Cup, 25th September 1963 (won 7-1)
- **First match at Emirates Stadium: v Ajax Amsterdam, Friendly, 22nd July 2006 (won 2-1)**
- First trophy: London Senior Cup v St. Bartholomew's Hospital (6-0) at the Kennington Oval, 7th March 1891 (six

months before turning professional)

- **First major trophy: FA Cup v Huddersfield (2-0) at Wembley, 25th Apr 1930**
- First southern club in the Football League: Admitted to Second Division in 1893
- **First Football League meeting between London clubs: Chelsea v Arsenal at Stamford Bridge, 2nd Nov 1907**
- First time players wore numbers on their backs in a Football League match: Arsenal v Sheff Weds, 25th Aug 1928
- **First time players wore squad numbers and names on their backs in a competitive English match: Arsenal v Sheff Weds, League Cup final, Wembley, 18th April 1993**
- First hat trick on full league debut: Ian Wright, v Southampton, First Division, 28th Sept 1991
- **First club to amass £100,000 gate receipts in a season: 1934/35**
- First film to be set at a football ground: *The Arsenal Stadium Mystery*, 1939
- **First match broadcast on radio: Arsenal v Sheffield United, 27th Jan 1927, transmitted on the BBC, Charlie Buchan's goal being the first on live radio commentary**
- First live football broadcast on television anywhere: Arsenal First Team v Arsenal Reserves, 16th Sept 1937
- parts of the specially arranged match were transmitted.
- **First ever game to be shown on the BBC's *Match of the Day* highlights programme: Liverpool v Arsenal, 22 Aug 1964**
- First footballer in the world to be transferred for more than £10,000: David Jack, from Bolton to Arsenal, 1928 (£10,890)
- **First team in the 20th century to participate in three consecutive F.A. Cup finals: Arsenal (1978-1980)**
- First team to win a League Championship on Goals Scored: Arsenal 1989 (level on points with Liverpool)
- **First overseas manager to win the title in England: Arsène Wenger, 1998**
- First capped Arsenal player: Caesar Jenkyns (for Wales v Scotland, 21st Mar 1896)
- **First capped Arsenal player for England: Jimmy Ashcroft (v Ireland, 17th Feb 1906)**
- First Arsenal player to captain England: David Jack, 1930
- **First Arsenal players to play in a World Cup: Dave Bowen and Jack Kelsey (for Wales v Hungary, 8th June 1958)**
- First Arsenal players to play in a World Cup for England: Graham Rix and Kenny Sansom (v France, 16th June 1982)
- **First Arsenal players to play in a World Cup final: Emmanuel Petit and Patrick Vieira (as substitute) for France v Brazil (12th July 1998)**
- First British side to defeat Real Madrid at the Bernabéu: 1-0 (UEFA Champions League second round first leg, 21st Feb 2006)
- **First team from London to reach the Champions League final: in 2006**